"I loved this book! The acceptanc[...] approach to overcoming stress and [...] the most groundbreaking and powerful approach I have ever encountered. Blonna's strategies are truly life-changing. I highly recommend this book."

—Lyn Kelley, Ph.D., LMFT, CPC, president of GROW Training Institute, Inc., and professional speaker, writer, coach, and consultant

"Like no other book available on stress, this volume both embraces what was useful about the traditional literature on stress and takes the reader into unexpected and powerful new territory. You will never think the same way about your stress again."

—Steven C. Hayes, Ph.D., Foundation Professor of Psychology at the University of Nevada and author of *Get Out of Your Mind and Into Your Life*

"In *Stress Less, Live More*, Blonna distills ACT into a useable stress management program. People looking for a natural and reasonable approach to reducing stress and increasing valued living will be drawn to this book."

—Kevin L. Polk, Ph.D., clinical psychologist and ACT trainer

STRESS LESS
live more

how acceptance &
commitment therapy
can help you live a
busy yet balanced life

RICHARD BLONNA, ED.D.

New Harbinger Publications, Inc.

Publisher's Note

This publication is designed to provide accurate and authoritative information in regard to the subject matter covered. It is sold with the understanding that the publisher is not engaged in rendering psychological, financial, legal, or other professional services. If expert assistance or counseling is needed, the services of a competent professional should be sought.

Distributed in Canada by Raincoast Books

Copyright © 2010 by Richard Blonna
New Harbinger Publications, Inc.
5674 Shattuck Avenue
Oakland, CA 94609
www.newharbinger.com

Acquired by Tesilya Hanauer; Cover design by Amy Shoup; Edited by Jean M. Blomquist; Text design by Tracy Carlson

Library of Congress Cataloging-in-Publication Data

Blonna, Richard.
  Stress less, live more : how acceptance and commitment therapy can help you live a busy yet balanced life / Richard Blonna.
      p. cm.
  Includes bibliographical references.
  ISBN 978-1-57224-709-3
  1. Stress (Psychology) 2. Stress management. 3. Acceptance and commitment therapy.
I. Title.
  BF575.S75B577 2010
  158.1--dc22

                    2009052773

12 11 10   10 9 8 7 6 5 4 3 2 1   First printing

I dedicate this book to Trudy Boyle, helper extraordinaire.

Contents

Dear Reader,

Welcome to New Harbinger Publications. New Harbinger is dedicated to publishing books based on acceptance and commitment therapy (ACT) and its application to specific areas. New Harbinger has a long-standing reputation as a publisher of quality, well-researched books for general and professional audiences.

Stress Less, Live More is a unique book. There are countless books on stress that focus on teaching readers ways of managing or reducing stress. Yet most people fail in their attempts at stress management, because they confuse managing stress with eliminating it. This book shows that this approach is doomed to fail, because you can't eliminate all of your stress; it is part of life. You also can't eliminate stress by trying to avoid it. When you avoid difficult issues because you're trying to escape the pain and suffering that goes along with pursuing your goals, you limit your potential for growth and long-term life satisfaction.

This book presents an entirely new way of looking at stress, as a holistic interaction between a person and a potential stressor. When you start to view stress this way, you will no longer see it as something that just happens to you and is beyond your ability to manage. Instead, you'll begin to view your stress as something that has a lot to do with what your mind tells you about potential stressors. This is very consistent with an ACT approach to understanding psychological problems in general. This book uses ACT to help you reexamine your desire to control, avoid, and eliminate stressful thoughts, beliefs, mental images, and emotions, while encouraging you to control what you can control—that is, to behave in ways that will take you closer to the life you want, despite feeling bad. The book helps you connect with what is going on in your body and mind, accept those experiences without getting all tangled up in them, and continue to move forward and take valued action.

What makes this book unique is its focus on how to live a purposeful life. Rather than drifting through life aimlessly, you choose actions based on clear and realistic goals you set for yourself. Your values, goals, and actions all come together when you live a purposeful life. The book will show you how this relates to stress in several ways. The author invites you to do a variety of engaging, practical, experiential exercises that will bring the chapters alive and make their content relevant to your particular life situation. For instance, several exercises will help you identify your core values and examine how they relate to your chosen purpose in life. You will learn to minimize the games and roles you play so that you can focus on living the life you value most dearly. When you do this, you take a big step toward reducing your stress. What you learn from this book will help you manage your stress in a different way, one that's more useful and more functional. It will fundamentally enrich your life, reaching far beyond the focus on stress.

As part of New Harbinger's commitment to publishing books based on sound, scientific, clinical research, we oversee all prospective books for the Acceptance and Commitment Therapy Series. Serving as series editors, we comment on proposals and offer guidance as needed, and use a gentle hand in making suggestions regarding the content, depth, and scope of each book.

Books in the Acceptance and Commitment Therapy Series:

- Have an adequate database, appropriate to the strength of the claims being made.

- Are theoretically coherent. They will fit with the ACT model and underlying behavioral principles as they have evolved at the time of writing.

- Orient the reader toward unresolved empirical issues.

- Do not overlap needlessly with existing volumes.

- Avoid jargon and unnecessary entanglement with proprietary methods, leaving ACT work open and available.

- Keep the focus always on what is good for the reader.

- Support the further development of the field.

- Provide information in a way that is of practical use to readers.

These guidelines reflect the values of the broader ACT community. You'll see all of them packed into this book. This series is meant to offer information that can truly be helpful, and to alleviate human suffering by offering a better approach.

Sincerely,

—Georg H. Eifert, Ph.D., John Forsyth, Ph.D.,
Steven C. Hayes, Ph.D., and Robyn Walser, Ph.D.

Acknowledgments

Sometimes life is like a puzzle with a key piece missing. That one missing piece keeps everything from falling into place. You know that if you can just find that piece, you can move forward and everything will fit together and work out fine. You search and search for the piece, coming back to the puzzle several times until you finally find it—and just as predicted, everything else falls into place beautifully.

ACT was the missing piece in the stress management puzzle for me. I'd spent the better part of the last twenty-five years crafting a framework for helping people manage their stress and then refining and refining it, trying to assemble all of the components in a meaningful way. There was always one piece missing, however—one that would make all of the others fit and work together seamlessly.

When I found ACT, I knew instantly that it was the missing piece. It was the last thing I needed to make my framework fit together and make sense to my students and clients. After reading my first article about Steven Hayes and ACT, I knew that there was a book in my head that needed to be written so I could share my ideas with others.

I am eternally grateful to Trudy Boyle for taking the time to think about me and send that article my way. Thanks, Trudy—it was the missing piece in my puzzle. Without you, my life would be on a different trajectory and this book would not exist.

Next I'd like to thank Steven Hayes for his hard work and dedication to creating and promoting ACT. He has worked tirelessly for the last two decades to test the scientific underpinnings of ACT, apply it in his work with clients, and share his findings with fellow researchers, clinicians, and students. He is instrumental in developing the Association for Contextual

Behavioral Science (ACBS) and using it as a platform to bring ACT to millions of people worldwide. Thanks, Steve, for your herculean efforts, as well as your help and kind words regarding this project.

I'd like to thank the "wild man" of ACT, Kevin Polk, for his mentoring. When I found his name listed on the ACBS website as a trainer and someone who provides supervision for ACT practitioners, I had no idea he was such a dynamo and would make learning ACT so much fun. Kevin taught me how to adopt an ACT view of the world and how to simplify this complex therapeutic approach and use it in my work with students and clients. Thanks, Kevin, for your caring, humor, and support, and for teaching me ACT. I definitely would not be here without you.

I'd like to thank Linda Anderson Krech and Gregg Krech, my spiritual mentors from the ToDo Institute in Vermont. I continue to find new applications for the information and skills I learned under their tutelage. Gregg and Linda, thanks for continuing to bring the Japanese therapies to thousands of people each year.

Next I want to thank Matt McKay, the founder and publisher of New Harbinger Publications, for taking the time to meet with me face-to-face and listen to my proposal for this book. Matt supported the project from the beginning and gave me the green light to refine the proposal and get it submitted. Thanks, Matt, for believing in me and giving me the chance to enter the world of self-help publishing.

Tesilya Hanauer, Jess Beebe, and Jean Blomquist, my editors at New Harbinger, taught me how to stop writing like an academician and start crafting a manuscript that would appeal to a broad spectrum of readers. Under their guidance, I gradually learned how to tailor my writing to this new audience. Thanks, Tesilya, Jess, and Jean, for your patience, guidance, help, and encouragement. All of these things motivated me to keep writing. Thanks also for your help in shaping the book. Thank you to Tracy McFadin and Tracy Carlson for fine-tuning the final manuscript with your excellent proofreading and production/design skills. This is definitely a better book than the original one that I proposed. I think you crafted a wonderful book!

I'd like to thank my friends and reviewers Gary Verhorn, Debbie Mindlin, Ken Horvath, and Heidi Blonna. Your insights and suggestions greatly improved the manuscript and kept me on target when my writing strayed off course or my ideas were not clear and understandable (which was often). Thanks for your unwavering support.

In addition to being my friend and reviewer, I'd also like to thank my wife, Heidi, for understanding how to give me both space and support at the same time. Sometimes she had to use ACT on me when my outdated personal scripts about being a husband got in the way of the reality of being a writer. Thanks, Hon, for your sacrifices and unconditional support.

Introduction

Chances are you bought this book because at least one of the following things is true about you: (1) you have a lot of responsibilities and demands on your life and your time, (2) your mind is constantly working overtime trying to keep track of these demands and responsibilities, (3) your body feels so tightly wound up that sometimes you feel as if you're going to explode, (4) you've already spent a considerable amount of money, time, and energy on other stress-related books, treatments, and self-help approaches, or (5) your struggles to avoid, control, or eliminate your stress just aren't working. If the stress profile I've created seems to fit, don't despair—help is on the way!

As a college professor, writer, and national certified counselor (NCC), certified professional coach (CPC), and certified health education specialist (CHES), I've studied stress management and worked with students and clients for over twenty-five years. I've developed an eclectic, health and wellness–based approach to stress management that incorporates hardy health habits, traditional coping strategies (diaphragmatic breathing, meditation, and others), management of illogical thinking, and constructive living skills derived from Zen Buddhist teachings.

About three years ago, I received an article from Trudy Boyle, a friend of mine who was the director of the Constructive Living and Learning Centre in Vancouver, British Columbia, Canada. It was about a man named Steve Hayes who had undertaken a miraculous journey from the depths of despair and mental illness to the founding of a new form of psychotherapy—acceptance and commitment therapy (ACT)—that was sweeping the nation and the world. I was fascinated with the story of Steve Hayes and the development of ACT, and I began to read everything I could on the subject.

One year later, my research led me to the website of the Association for Contextual and Behavioral Science (ACBS), the parent professional organization that represents ACT researchers and practitioners from around the world. The organization provides information, resources, and a directory of ACT trainers around the world. Seeking additional postdoctoral training in ACT, I contacted Dr. Kevin Polk, a noted ACT trainer and psychotherapist working in Maine with military veterans suffering from post-traumatic stress disorder (PTSD) and other problems. After talking with Kevin for five minutes, I knew I wanted to work with him to learn as much as I could about ACT. Kevin instantly came off as the kind of person I could relax around and just be myself with. He exuded a passion for ACT, a down-to-earth approach to training practitioners, and a dry sense of humor that seemed to be a good fit for me. I knew he'd give me the training and professional supervision I craved and needed to apply ACT to my work with clients and students.

Kevin is the official "wild man" of ACT. His "ACT Gone Wild" workshops are noted for their high energy, spontaneity, and creative applications of ACT principles for counselors and therapists working in a variety of settings. Under Kevin's tutelage, I learned how to apply basic ACT therapeutic principles to my work in stress management teaching and counseling. From my first day working with Kevin, I knew that I needed to write a book that integrated ACT principles into stress management. ACT is so powerful and such a good fit for the way I teach people to manage their stress that I felt driven to write this book. I knew I couldn't rest until I did. It just seemed like the next logical leg on my journey to bring ACT to people who would benefit from it—people like you.

My approach to stress management combines ACT with other proven stress management principles and practices. It goes beyond quick fixes and gives you a framework for lifelong relief from excess stress. You notice I said "excess" stress. This is intentional because I don't want to mislead you. I can't teach you how to eliminate or control 100 percent of your stress. To be alive is to be stressed. My goal in writing this book is to help you minimize the amount of stress you experience and learn how to manage the rest.

Many of the stress management strategies in this book are cognitive in nature—that is, they use the power of your mind to change the way you think about potential stressors and your ability to cope with them. If you can change the way you think about potential stressors (starting with labeling them "potential" stressors), you can defuse their power and keep them from becoming actual stressors. ACT is a perfect fit for rethinking potential stressors and coping because it's based on the ability of your mind and your language (the actual words you use to describe things) to influence your stress.

An ACT view of stress supports my "transactional" way of defining stress. I'll show you how the transaction between a potential stressor (traffic, bills, taxes, public speaking, or whatever) and a stress response (racing heart, dry mouth, anxious feelings, and so on) is determined by what you tell yourself about the situation. ACT can help you to look at potential stressors more realistically and to more accurately gauge the threat they pose as well as your ability to cope with them. It can harness the power of your mind to keep your potential stressors from turning into actual ones.

In this book, I won't ask you to cut back and do less. Nor will I ask you to give up the activities and pursuits that you love and are passionate about. Instead I'll show you how to gain more control of your time and the demands on it. I'll help you learn how to look at your responsibilities in a different way and set priorities that are consistent with your goals and what you truly value in life. I won't force you to change your lifestyle or personality. Indeed, part of the key to managing your stress is accepting who you are, being yourself, and letting the person you are shine through.

A major focus of this book is helping you to understand how your mind works during stressful encounters. I'll show you why your attempts to avoid, control, and eliminate stress don't work. And, more importantly, I'll show you how to manage your stress by applying ACT principles and practices and by using the power of your mind and body working together.

Are you ready to learn how to manage your stress? If so, let's begin our journey by looking at a new way to define stress, in chapter 1.

CHAPTER 1

What Is Stress?

If you ask ten people to define stress, they'll probably define it ten different ways. George says, "Stress is feeling like a pressure cooker that's about to explode." Diane describes it as something in the environment, some external "stimulus" or trigger: "Stress is taxes." Scott puts the two together: "It's the muscle tension I get in my neck when I think about how I'm going to pay my monthly bills and still save for my kid's college education." Other friends might view stress more holistically—as part of a larger whole—and describe it as the emotional distress they feel when their lives are out of balance. For Tina, stress is "being a mother and not having any time to myself." For Rob, it's "being in a failed relationship and feeling listless and emotionally flat," and for Lynne, it's "needing surgery and feeling trapped in a dead-end job that doesn't have health benefits."

Though these people's definitions reflect their own experience of stress, each of these ways of defining stress is incomplete. At the same time, however, each contains a nugget of truth regarding the nature of stress. In reality, stress combines elements of each of these definitions. To understand the true nature of stress requires combining the pieces to create a new, more comprehensive way of defining stress.

A NEW WAY TO DEFINE STRESS

In my college textbook, *Coping with Stress in a Changing World* (2007), I define *stress* as "a holistic transaction between an individual and a potential stressor resulting in a stress response" (12). The four key components of this definition (holistic, transaction, potential stressor, and stress response) are drawn from the fields of health, psychology, and physiology respectively.

Each field represents a rich historical tradition of theory and practice that's contributed to an understanding of stress and how to manage it. In the next section, I'll spend a little time explaining a couple of things about the key aspects of the definition and why it's such a good fit with an ACT view of stress.

A Holistic Approach

The term *holistic* comes from holistic health, a multifaceted way of viewing health. Your health can be your best ally in your efforts to manage your stress. It can provide the energy and support you need to assess, understand, accept, and cope with stressful situations. The holistic health and wellness movements developed in response to traditional models of health that defined it as a state of mental, physical, and social well-being. The pioneers of the holistic health and wellness movements of the 1970s and '80s expanded the view of health to include the spiritual, environmental, and occupational dimensions (Dunn 1962; Ardell 1985). They also believed that mental health had two dimensions: the intellectual, which deals with thoughts and thinking, and the emotional, which deals with emotions and feeling. Finally, they felt that health wasn't a static state but rather an ever-changing process. In other words, your body, mind, spirit, relationships, and environment are constantly evolving and dynamic. To be effective, any comprehensive stress management program must also be dynamic, not static.

The Nature of Potential Stressors

A *potential stressor* is something, someone, or some situation that has the ability to threaten you or something that you value. It's crucial that you realize that a stressor is really only a *potential* stressor until you feel threatened by it and feel that you can't cope with it. People, places, and situations are not inherently stressful to everyone in all circumstances. The whole idea of *universal stressors* (stressors that stress everyone all the time) is an outdated concept. The notion of universal stressors came out of the research of Thomas Holmes and Richard Rahe (1967). They coined the term *life events* to refer to universal experiences (marriage, divorce, moving, losing your job, and so on) that were capable of triggering a stress response. Holmes and Rahe found that if you had accumulated too many life-events points in the previous year, you had an increased risk of suffering a mental or physical illness. Their research, however, never factored in what people like you might think about these events or your ability to cope with them.

More recent life-events research has shown that factoring in your thinking (that is, your perception of the event) and your ability to cope with a potential stressor can actually defuse it as a stressor (DeLongis et al. 1982). Take the death of a loved one as an example. You could perceive the loss of a loved one as an unexpected and tragic loss, a major threat to your well-being, and something that you just can't cope with. You could also perceive it as an expected outcome, a blessing in disguise, and something that—while painful to experience—you're able to cope with. Your ability to cope with the loss also varies, and it is influenced by a host of things, ranging from your relationship to your loved one to the support system you have in place to help you through this loss. Your ability to cope is also influenced by the nature of the loved one's death. If the person was in a lot of pain and was suffering from a terminal illness such as cancer, you might view their death differently than if they passed suddenly in their sleep for no apparent reason or if they were the victim of a violent crime. In essence, even the death of a loved one—the most stressful event possible according to Holmes and Rahe—is not a universal stressor to all people under all circumstances.

Since stressors are relative and not universal, it's possible to alter your relationship to them and how you view them. ACT can help you change the way you view potential stressors. It can teach you how to step back and distance yourself from them so you can assess them and your ability to cope with them more accurately. The whole idea of what should be stressful to you is often a tangled web of objective information, your past experiences and learning, and social expectations (how other people think you should react). ACT can help you sort through all of this and make up your own mind about what's stressful to you.

The Stress Response

A *stress response* is a chain reaction of physiological events that occurs in your body once you feel threatened and unable to cope with a potential stressor. Once this happens, your brain sends messages throughout your body via nerve transmissions and hormones that switch on a complex response designed to mobilize energy to help you fight or flee from the stressor.

Hans Selye (1956), the father of modern stress research, described his view of the stress response in his "general adaptation syndrome" (GAS).

The GAS has three stages: (1) alarm, (2) resistance, and (3) exhaustion. The three stages are progressive. In other words, when you're stressed, the response moves from alarm to resistance and eventually to exhaustion if you don't eliminate the source of stress or cope with it effectively.

The *alarm* stage of GAS is also known as the *fight-or-flight response*. During the alarm response, your body is primed to either confront the stressor (fight) or avoid it (flight). Alarm is a high-intensity but short-lived response designed to get you out of harm's way in a hurry.

Selye found that when he exposed his laboratory animals to chronic, long-term stressors, they couldn't sustain the alarm response indefinitely. It was simply too intense to maintain this high-intensity response for long periods. Instead they adapted to the stimuli by shifting out of alarm to a lower-level but more complex stress response called *resistance*. Humans respond in a similar way. During resistance, your body produces a variety of hormones, salts, and sugars to supply the energy you need to resist the demands of the stressor and keep all of your body systems (breathing, circulation, and so on) in balance.

Exhaustion results from the gradual wearing down of your body during the resistance stage. Selye believed that all living organisms have a finite amount of energy stored in the body to adapt to stressors—in other words, we can't resist indefinitely.

Selye also believed that each person has different weak links that are most susceptible to exhaustion. Your weak link could be any body part or system that bears the brunt of resistance. So your weak link could be, for example, your lower back muscles or thyroid gland, or perhaps your muscular or respiratory system. Prior to breaking down completely, your weak link will begin to malfunction and send you warning signs that you're experiencing wear and tear. For example, if your weak link is your lower back, you might experience chronic lower back pain for a time before it seized up into spasms (representing the exhaustion stage). A key to effective stress management is paying attention to these and other warning signs before they result in exhaustion.

The Transactional Nature of Stress

Viewing stress as a "transaction" comes primarily from the work of Richard S. Lazarus and Suzanne Folkman (1984) and their study of the psychology of stress and coping. A *stress transaction* is how you view a potential stressor and your ability to cope with it once you're exposed to it. Once you're exposed to a potential stressor, your brain assesses two things: (1) whether the potential stressor is threatening or harmful to you or has caused you to lose something important, and (2) your ability to cope with it.

Potential stressors can be threatening in many different ways. They can be life-threatening, as in the case of being confronted by a mugger. They can be financially threatening, such as hearing that you might lose your job. Or your ego or social status can be threatened. Any kind of threat, including loss and harm, can trigger a stress response. While threat is something you anticipate can happen, loss and harm have already occurred. For example, the loss of a loved one is a common source of stress. If you broke your leg or tore a ligament in your knee, this harmful event could be a source of stress for you. Threat can also transform into harm or loss if the potentially threatening event turns out to be genuine.

Assessing your ability to cope with something is pretty clear-cut. If you feel you can handle a potential stressor, you usually can draw on some strategies you've used in the past that you think will work for you with the current potential stressor. This is especially true if you've experienced something similar to it in the past and coped with it successfully.

Your assessment as to whether you can cope or not determines whether or not the potential stressor triggers a stress response. If you perceive something as threatening and feel you're unable to cope with it, your brain will trigger a stress response. If the potential stressor is a threat to you but you feel that you can cope with it, your brain won't trigger a stress response. Richard S. Lazarus and Suzanne Folkman (1984) also found a positive outcome of a transaction with a potential stressor, which they called a "challenge response." The challenge response represents a clear break from the prior ways of viewing stress.

The Challenge Response

Challenge is an energy-mobilizing response that is accompanied by positive emotions. Challenge mobilizes energy the same way the stress response does during fight or flight. Unlike the stress response, however, the challenge response is short-lived and does not shift into resistance.

The stress response, unlike the challenge response, is always accompanied by negative emotions related to feeling threatened. When you're stressed, feelings such as fear, anxiety, anger, and hostility, along with feeling threatened, cause your stress response to shift from alarm to resistance (Frankenhaeuser 1983). (Please bear with me for a moment as we discuss some of the theory around the challenge and stress responses. Then I'll give you an example in the next section that will clarify what we're talking about here.) In addition, new ways of measuring stress hormones have documented that cortisol is the key hormone that keeps your stress response alive—that is, cortisol, which is secreted during the resistance stage of the stress response, prolongs the stress response by triggering your liver to convert protein and fat into energy to fuel the stress response. However, studies also show that cortisol is not secreted when you are challenged (Frankenhaeuser 1983).

When you're challenged, you also have on a different view of potential stressors. You focus on the positive things that can result from taking on a potential stressor. When you feel challenged, you look at a situation for its growth potential or for what you might gain from the challenge. For example, you use challenge when getting psyched up to give a presentation at work or to accomplish a task that excites you and gives you the opportunity to showcase your talents.

Like the fight-or-flight response, challenge involves the rapid mobilization of energy needed to confront the potential stressor. The difference is that, even though this energy mobilization is as intense as the energy resulting from the stress response, it's short term and dissipates once you meet the challenge.

When you're challenged, you don't view a potential stressor as a threat because you don't feel threatened by it. Instead you feel eagerness, excitement, and exhilaration rather than the negative feelings that are part of feeling threatened. You also feel confident in your ability to cope with the challenge. ACT can help you learn how your mind works when appraising the threat, harm, or loss posed by potential stressors and your ability to cope with it. With the ACT skills you'll learn in this book, you'll begin to harness the power of your mind to change threats into challenges. ACT can help you accept the things you can't control about challenges and keep moving forward to fulfill your goals.

THE ROLE OF SPACE AND TIME

I'd like to mention one last thing about the nature of any holistic stress transaction. Your evaluation of a potential stressor as threatening or not is always influenced by the time and place in which you're exposed to the potential stressor, as well as by your overall health status at this point. This is why you'll evaluate the same potential stressor differently the next time you're exposed to it. Not only will you be exposed to it at a different time and under different circumstances, *you* will be a different person and have the benefit of experience on your side. You can learn how to draw on this experience in a positive way. ACT can help you do this by accepting the emotions and thoughts associated with the new exposure to the potential stressor and defusing from your outdated and inflexible ways of looking at it and dealing with it.

Let's use taking an important examination as an example. Imagine that you're a senior in college majoring in criminal justice and you are applying for a job as a police officer in a neighboring town. You're a solid student and have earned mostly A's and B's in all of your college courses. Your college record and degree qualify you for the educational requirement needed to enter the police academy. In addition to the educational requirements, you'll have to take a written exam and a fitness test.

You feel qualified to take the written exam and view it as a challenge, a chance to prove yourself. You take the written part of the entrance exam and pass it with flying colors, earning one of the top three scores. Unfortunately the physical fitness part of the exam is a totally different experience. It involves a twelve-minute run and tests of strength, agility, and flexibility. You dread the fitness test. You hate to run and have been too busy with school to work out consistently the past few months. You perceive this part of the test as a real threat to all of your future plans.

Needless to say, you don't do well on the fitness test. The run is a dismal failure and the thoughts of this carry into the other components of the exam. You don't earn a high enough score to pass the fitness test and therefore don't pass the exam. You're denied entrance to the police academy and your dreams are dashed.

Now fast-forward six months. You're now finished with college and are working part-time as an attendant at a local gym so you'll have better access to a high-quality training facility. You're getting ready to take another fitness test at a police academy in a different town. You've already taken the written part of the entrance examination and passed with the second-highest score.

Unlike six months ago, you're focused and have a positive mind-set for the fitness test. You've been working out faithfully six days a week, running and lifting weights. You're still afraid and feeling anxious about the fitness test, but you accept these emotions and say to yourself, *It's normal to experience these feelings when facing such an important test.* On the day of the race, you're confident and looking forward to the opportunity to prove to yourself that you can pass the fitness test. You don't finish with the fastest time, but you're fast enough to pass this part of the test. This boosts your confidence and you approach the remaining events with a calm confidence. You pass the remaining parts of the fitness test and are invited to enter the police academy.

In both of these scenarios, you were exposed to the same potential stressor, having to pass the physical fitness part of the police academy exam. In the first scenario, you went into it unprepared and full of self-defeating thoughts and troubling feelings. You didn't know how to handle these thoughts and feelings, and they got the best of you. Your negative appraisal of the potential stressor turned it into an actual stressor, and this made passing the test even harder.

In the second scenario, you were exposed to the same potential stressor but handled it entirely differently. You had the benefit of having already experienced a similar test and could go back in your mind and analyze what went wrong. You used this information to set goals and do whatever you could to prepare for the test. You still felt anxious and worried, but on the day of the second fitness test, you appraised it entirely differently. You accepted your initial negative thoughts and feelings but added new, positive ones. This changed your mind-set and made the test a challenge and a chance to prove yourself. Rather than creating stress, your brain triggered a challenge response, complete with the energy and positive thinking you needed to succeed. You carried your success on the run over to success on the other parts of the fitness test.

With practice, you can learn how to transform potential stressors into challenges and harness the power of your body and mind. Throughout this book, I'll give you examples of how to apply ACT principles and practices and other stress management techniques to turn your stressors into challenges. In the next chapter, you'll learn all about ACT and see how it can become the cornerstone of your stress-management plan.

CHAPTER 2

What Is ACT?

Acceptance and commitment therapy (ACT) is a form of psychotherapy based on cognitive behavior therapy (CBT) and relational frame therapy (RFT; Hayes, Barnes-Holmes, and Roche 2001). You don't have to understand the other therapies that ACT is based on, however, to be able to use ACT in dealing with your stress.

An underlying premise of ACT is that stress and mental suffering occur when you become rigid and inflexible in your thinking and get stuck in a rut. ACT refers to this as becoming "psychologically inflexible." ACT helps you become more psychologically flexible, get unstuck, and behave in ways that support your goals and what you value in life. Getting unstuck and developing greater psychological flexibility starts with understanding the relationships among your self-talk (the inner dialogue that goes on in your mind when you're confronted with a potential stressor), your emotions, and your behavior.

ACT looks at the usefulness of your thoughts, emotions, and behavior in specific situations, or "contexts," that relate to your values and goals. To help determine what's useful and what isn't, ACT asks you to consider this basic question: Are these thoughts and feelings helping me act in ways that are consistent with my values and goals? If your answer is yes, you can accept them and continue to move forward. If the answer is no, you can dismiss those thoughts because they don't help you live out your values and goals.

ACT operates from the premise that your thoughts don't all have equal weight. You might say there are three kinds of thoughts: (1) helpful, (2) minimally important or silly, and (3) illogical, negative, and self-destructive. First, helpful thoughts support your values and help you meet your goals. These thoughts usually help you manage your stress as well. For example, as you work through a difficult task you might find yourself thinking, *Boy, this is harder than I thought it would be. I'd better give myself extra time to complete it.* This kind of thought helps you stay focused and accept the hard work involved in meeting your goals. Second, some thoughts—those of minimal importance and those that are pretty silly—can easily be dismissed. These thoughts usually don't play a part in your stress one way or another. For example, imagine you're at work and you find yourself thinking about having sex with your partner. You realize that your thoughts have drifted away from your work and onto your sexual fantasies. You simply acknowledge this has happened and say to yourself, *I better get my mind back on my work or I'll never finish this project.* The third and final category of thoughts is the illogical, negative, and self-destructive ones that make it difficult for you to meet your goals and live the kind of life you want. These types of thoughts also contribute to your feeling threatened and unable to cope, and make it difficult for you to manage your stress. For example, imagine that one of your goals is to go back to college and finish your degree. You really value earning a college degree, but you had to drop out five years ago because of financial difficulties. Those are now behind you, and you're ready and able to reenter college. Every time you get set to fill out the application and reenroll, you find your mind telling you things like *You're too old to go back, You'll never finish college after dropping out for five years,* or *You'll never be able to go back and pick up where you left off.* These negative thoughts are not based on any logical evidence, yet your mind believes them, and this creates a barrier that keeps you from enrolling and making progress toward your goal of finishing college and earning your degree.

ACCEPTANCE, COMMITMENT, AND THERAPY

The two main components of ACT are acceptance and commitment. Each plays a key role in helping you stay true to your values as you take steps to meet your goals. As you'll see in the rest of this chapter, ACT is based on helping you live a life that's consistent with what you value and the goals you set for yourself.

The Acceptance Component of ACT

Acceptance has three aspects: (1) becoming more mindful of your thoughts, emotions, and actions; (2) understanding how your thoughts, emotions, and actions support or oppose your values and goals; and (3) understanding that it's impossible to control, eliminate, or avoid painful thoughts and emotions and trying to do so actually increases your suffering. Let's take a quick look at each of these aspects.

First, *mindfulness* is a thread that runs through every chapter of this book. It means paying attention to each moment, and being more aware of the internal (what's going on in your body and mind) and external events in your life.

Second, to understand how your thoughts, emotions, and actions either support or oppose your values and goals, you first need to clarify them. Later in this chapter, I'll introduce you to "values clarification" to help you start thinking about your values and how they relate to your stress.

And third, probably the most important aspect of acceptance—and the one that makes it the key component of ACT—is the fact that when you try to avoid, control, or eliminate painful thoughts and feelings, they actually worsen. One of the things that attracted me to ACT as a form of therapy was the solid research that supports this finding. ACT isn't based on speculation or mysticism. It's based on solid psychological research that studies the relationships among language, emotions, and behavior (Luoma, Hayes, and Walser 2007). This research shows that focusing your attention and self-talk on trying to avoid, control, or eliminate painful thoughts and feelings actually increases your suffering. Russ Harris (2007) calls this the "happiness trap," the misguided belief that the goal of life should be the elimination of all pain and suffering. While such a goal sounds good initially, you'll see in the following chapters that 24/7 happiness is not only impossible, it's also counterproductive and actually causes stress.

The Commitment Component of ACT

The *commitment* component of ACT helps you commit to actions that are consistent with your values and goals. When you commit to something, you pledge to yourself to follow through with your plans. Commitment training teaches you how to stick to your plans while coexisting with your pain and suffering. It shows you that you don't have to eliminate your painful thoughts and feelings in order to move forward and get on with your life. People often confuse pain and suffering with stress; ACT teaches you not to. As long as you realize that it's normal to have painful thoughts and feelings and to suffer, you'll feel able to cope with these issues. As you've seen in chapter 1, stress comes from feeling threatened and unable to cope. You need not feel threatened by pain and suffering; they're as much a part of your life as the air you breathe and the sunlight that streams through your window.

The Therapeutic Component of ACT

The therapeutic part of ACT is based on the latest research of how your mind really works when it processes stressful thoughts, feelings, and mental images. It's very different from other therapeutic approaches that have you spend months and years analyzing your past or trying to change your thinking and feeling before you can make any progress and live the life that you want for yourself. You'll see in the coming pages how ACT can help you immediately by teaching you how to harness the power of your mind to help you manage your stress.

HOW YOU LEARN ABOUT STRESS

Steven Hayes and his colleagues (2001) at the University of Nevada at Reno found that when you learn something, you learn it in relation to other things specific to that time and place. This implies that the *context* of your learning is as important as the *content* of it. For example, your current thoughts, emotions, and behavior about a potential stressor are related to their original frames of reference (or what psychologists call "relational frames") from your past in which you initially learned about this stressor. The way you respond to this current potential stressor can be influenced entirely by your brain's ability to use information from that original frame of reference. Your mind uses information from previous relational frames as the basis for assessing the threat posed by current potential stressors. In addition, your mind can carry this one step further and use the same previous information to jump ahead and project an infinite number of future situations involving this and similar potential stressors. Your mind's ability to use the past and present to jump ahead and anticipate future problems is the basis for a lot of your worry and anxiety.

Let me use fear of public speaking as an example of how this process works. Imagine that you're like many people who are stressed out by public speaking. Your boss tells you that tomorrow you have to address your work group (about one hundred people) regarding the status of a project you're in charge of. After hearing this, you start to feel severe anxiety and the following physical symptoms: sweating, muscle tension, and dizziness. Accompanying these emotional and physical symptoms, you find yourself thinking thoughts like these: *I'll just die if I have to give this speech, I'll fall apart right on that stage, I'm the world's worst public speaker,* or *I'm such an idiot for feeling like this.*

Your first response to this situation might be to try to avoid the situation by asking your boss if someone else could address the group. You can't figure out why something as simple as presenting information to your colleagues can cause such emotional distress. To understand this better, you need to go back twenty-five years and look at an earlier frame of reference.

Imagine you're in your high school English class. You have to give a ten-minute speech about a book you read over the winter break. Even though this happened twenty-five years ago, you can close your eyes and remember the event as if it had happened yesterday. Even though you read the book, understood it completely, and enjoyed it immensely, when you stood in front of the class, you started sweating, your tongue felt three inches thick, your mouth went dry, and you froze, unable to utter a word. All of the other students laughed, and the teacher, after letting you suffer for what seemed like an eternity, dismissed you with a curt remark about being unprepared.

Since then, all of your thoughts, feelings, and actions about public speaking have been filtered through the original frame of reference (the relational frame) of that experience (the failed high school speaking assignment). In college, you agonized over every class that required public speaking. You avoided most of them by dropping out as soon as you learned of the public speaking requirement. Up until this point in your life and career, you've managed to avoid most of the situations that have required that you speak in public. At forty-two, you're very successful and accomplished in a number of different areas, yet twenty-five years removed from that initial experience, your fear of public speaking still haunts you. You still find yourself caught up in illogical thinking and negative self-talk that keeps you stuck in a rut that you wish you could get out of.

Why do things like this happen? One reason is that your past experiences—or frames of reference—always operate in the background of your brain. ACT views your brain as a 24/7 thinking and feeling machine. Like a computer, it constantly processes information and is capable of running multiple programs at the same time. These "programs" are your thoughts, personal scripts, mental images, and emotions. While you're familiar with thoughts, emotions, and mental images, let me take a moment to define what personal scripts are. *Personal scripts* are like scenes in a play. The play in this case is your life, and each script paints a picture of how you envision the scene is supposed to play out. You have personal scripts about everything from how your date tomorrow night will turn out to what will happen when you go in and ask your boss for a raise on Monday. Personal scripts, like thoughts, emotions, and mental images, are based in part on past relational frames. Like the operating system or virus checker programs on your computer's hard drive, your programs run in the background without you even realizing they're on. Like viruses that invade your computer, your illogical thoughts and negative self-talk can invade your programs, slow you down, or cause your brain (like your computer processor) to "freeze up" and not function. You've probably noticed, for example, that when you're really stressed, you just can't seem to think clearly, you feel jittery and tongue-tied, and sometimes you just shut down.

What can you do to get unstuck? Is there a way to break free from past frames of reference that no longer reflect who you are? How do you overcome these ghosts from your past that still haunt you? The bad news is that you probably have lots of negative relational frames from your past operating in the background of your mind that make it easy to get stuck now and then. The good news is that you don't have to spend a lot of time analyzing them, trying to undo them, or trying to figure them out in order to move forward and get out of your rut. You can live the life you want now while coexisting with them. Being able to coexist with past frames of reference that no longer reflect who you are is a hallmark of what ACT refers to as "psychological flexibility." In the next section, I'll show you how to develop greater psychological flexibility.

DEVELOPING PSYCHOLOGICAL FLEXIBILITY

As I mentioned earlier, ACT uses the term "psychological inflexibility" to explain what happens to you when you suffer from chronic stress and other emotional problems and get stuck in a rut. The reason psychological inflexibility causes you to get stuck is that it limits your ability to deal with potential stressors and other psychological threats in new and creative ways. When you're inflexible, it often seems that you have few, if any, options available to cope with or solve your problems. ACT identifies six key elements, called *core processes*, that contribute to your psychological inflexibility: (1) attachment to the conceptualized self, (2) cognitive fusion, (3) the dominance of outmoded scripts and learning, (4) experiential avoidance, (5) lack of clarity concerning values, and (6) inaction, impulsivity, and rigidity. These terms may sound a bit foreign, but as we take a closer look at them, I think you'll recognize at least some of them from your own life.

Attachment to the Conceptualized Self

Steve Hayes (2005) uses the term *conceptualized self* to refer to what most people think about when asked to describe themselves. Your conceptualized self describes you with statements that summarize and evaluate who you are and what you do. For example, if I asked you to describe yourself, you'd probably say things such as "I'm thirty-five years old," "I'm of average height," "I'm happily married," "I'm an architect," or "I'm kind and I'm lovable." These kinds of self-statements sum up who you are and how you measure up compared to some societal standard (intelligence, income, body composition, and so on). ACT refers to this way of describing yourself as *self-as-content*. In other words, you are the sum total of all of the things contained within you.

Your mind often attaches labels to pieces of your conceptualized self and creates stereotypes, or "shortcuts," to understanding and explaining who you really are. For example, imagine you went to a psychiatrist a while back and she diagnosed you with social phobia. From that point on, you began to view yourself as a social phobic. Being a social phobic, instead of being a person who is stressed by certain social situations, represents a totally different version of your conceptualized self. When you call yourself a social phobic, you *become* the illness. All of the stereotypes you associate with social phobia (having to avoid specific social situations, anticipating feeling anxious and near panic when forced to attend social functions, suffering physical symptoms such as shortness of breath, increased heart rate, and so on) now substitute for you, the person, who also happen to suffer from social phobia. This restricted way of viewing your self and the world around you limits your choices or options because it doesn't allow you to see everything clearly. When this happens, it limits your psychological flexibility and you get stuck.

One way to get unstuck when your conceptualized self limits your psychological flexibility is to tap into another type of self, your *observer self*. While your conceptualized self is also known as your self-as-content (viewing yourself as the content of your thoughts), your observer self is known as your *self-as-context*. You can think of your observer self as the perspective from which you view all of the content of your conceptualized self. The context in which all of your life plays out is the essential you. This is the "you" that has been here from the very beginning and transcends your life experience by being the one constant variable in your existence. This is the you who observed all of the challenges and stressors that make you who you are: your first day of school, your first date, your first failure, and the first time someone broke your heart or let you down. Your observer self has been the constant throughout all of these firsts and the hundreds of thousands of additional experiences you've had since then that make up the richness of your life. Learning to differentiate between your conceptualized and observer selves is a key component of learning how to use ACT to manage your stress. If you can view your self and your mind as the context in which your experiences play out rather than being the actual content itself, you can start to look at some of the content more objectively. So, instead of being a social phobic, you're a person who happens to get extremely stressed under certain social situations. In addition to this, however, you love medieval art, are a great cook, like to play crossword puzzles, and have a great dog named Sparky. You're the perspective out of which all of these things flow and are observed.

Adopting an observer's view of your self allows you to step back and impartially look at your mind as something that's capable of both profound wisdom and complete silliness. You can actually start to say things to yourself like *Boy, that was really a silly thought that my mind just told me.* This can defuse the power of what your mind tells you. In chapter 3, I'll show you how your mind gets you into trouble by having you buy into a host of myths regarding your thoughts and feelings. For now, just try to start thinking of your self as the perspective from which you view your mind's functioning rather than you being your mind.

Cognitive Fusion

When you call yourself a "social phobic" or identify with any other negative self-description (a loser, a loner, a neurotic, and so on) and you thereby become the problem, you *fuse* with that part of your conceptualized self. This is what ACT means by *cognitive fusion*. Your mind can fuse with all kinds of unhelpful thoughts, feelings, and images. When this happens, you view the world through this fused concept of reality rather than seeing the actual reality. Viewing the world this way limits what you allow yourself to see and experience. It's like wearing blinders that restrict your vision to what's right in front of you. Viewing the world this way puts limits on the options that might be available to you. When your concept of reality is limiting, as in the example of the person described as a "social phobic," you lose some of your psychological flexibility and get stuck.

Cognitive defusion is the process of separating your self from the unhelpful thoughts that create stress and keep you stuck. When you defuse from your unhelpful thoughts, you step back and observe them without judgment. You realize that they represent just a part of your conceptualized self, don't necessarily reflect reality, and don't have to be taken too seriously or acted upon if they aren't helpful in meeting your goals. When you can become an impartial observer of your unhelpful thoughts, and not take them as orders or having the equivalent weight of helpful thoughts, you can begin to lessen their influence. Like leaves on a stream in autumn, you can learn how to let them drift by as you observe them come and go.

One of my favorite defusion activities is called The Whiteboard. It's an excellent activity to use when you want to create distance between you and your unhelpful thoughts.

DEFUSION ACTIVITY: The Whiteboard

In order to do this activity, you'll need either a whiteboard or large pad of paper and some color markers.

The next time you're having painful, unhelpful thoughts that contribute to your stress and the feeling of being stuck, get out your whiteboard or large pad and markers. Pick up one of the markers and write this heading: Unhelpful Thoughts My Mind Is Telling Me About [whatever you're stuck about]. For example, "Unhelpful Thoughts My Mind Is Telling Me About Starting to Date Again" or "Unhelpful Thoughts My Mind Is Telling Me About Asking for a Raise." List all of the thoughts your mind is telling you about being stuck. For example, about dating again, you might find your mind telling you, *I'm too old to be doing this* or *I'll never find another person like my ex-wife*. Regarding asking for a raise, your mind might say things such as *I don't really need the money* or *I should be happy to just have a job.* Be sure to list all of your thoughts—no matter how crazy, silly, or inconsequential they might seem to be. When you're done, put down the marker and step back a few feet from the board or pad. Tell yourself, *These are merely my thoughts—they are not me. I am much more than these thoughts.* Feel the distance you have between you and these unhelpful thoughts. Try stepping back even farther to put more distance between you and these unhelpful thoughts.

How do these thoughts feel now?

By stepping back and observing your unhelpful thoughts from a distance, you get a different perspective on them. When you say to yourself, *My mind is telling me...*or *My mind is having the thought that...*, the unhelpful, painful thoughts no longer seem like a part of you. They're merely thoughts, something your brain is capable of cranking out nonstop all day long. Remember, not all of these thoughts are equally helpful in helping you move forward toward realizing your goals.

Dominance of Outmoded Scripts and Learning

Think back to the example in which I asked you to imagine that you avoid public speaking because you failed at it in high school. It's a perfect example of how fusing with outmoded scripts and previous learning continue to drive current behavior. I described personal scripts as being like scenes in the play of your life. Another way of putting it is that a script is really a story that your mind creates about some facet of your life related to your experience. For example, the script of a forty-two-year-old who is anxious about giving a presentation at work is probably something like this: *I'm just not a good public speaker. I never was, and it isn't something I can learn. I just don't have the ability to stand in front of a room and talk to people. Whenever I even think of public speaking, I get all nervous.* You have scripts running around in your mind about everything from sex to public speaking. These scripts are related to your age and developmental level. Some were developed as far back as early childhood, while others are as recent as last week. Some are helpful and tell you that you can cope with potential stressors and challenges that come your way. Others aren't helpful and stand in the way of your moving forward in life. A script becomes *outmoded* when it no longer represents who you are or is no longer helpful in meeting your goals and living a life that is true to what you value.

A key step in assessing whether a script is outmoded and unhelpful is being mindful and accepting of its existence. For example, imagine that one of your personal scripts revolves around having failed at your first attempt to open your own small business many years ago. Since this initial failure, you've had three other business ventures that did very well. Even though you have been very successful, your personal script related to business is filled with self-defeating statements and worry about your failure rather than your successes. A key step in continuing to move forward with future ventures is acknowledging that you still carry this negative script around even though it's no longer true. Once you're aware of its presence and acknowledge that it no longer holds true, you can begin to accept that you don't need to rid yourself of it in order to pursue your goals.

You get stuck when you miss or deny the presence of outmoded scripts that dominate your thinking and behavior. Sometimes you don't even realize this is happening because your mind has the ability to act as if it is on autopilot sometimes, performing activities such as driving without you even having to think about them. You can literally go through days where you lose track of time and details without even realizing this. A forty-two-year-old man who is still stuck in an outdated public speaking script, for example, doesn't allow himself to look at possible ways to develop his expertise in public speaking. He doesn't even acknowledge that this is an option anymore. Even though his avoidance of public speaking impacts his career negatively, he doesn't act on this: he just remains stuck.

Experiential Avoidance

Life is full of possibilities if you allow yourself to take advantage of them. *Experiential avoidance* gets you stuck because it works exactly the opposite way. When you avoid an experience because it makes you uncomfortable (such as public speaking), it limits your possibilities, making you less psychologically flexible. Always staying in your comfort zone is a safe way to live your life, but it can also contribute to your missing out on a lot of growth-enhancing experiences. Experiential avoidance is often linked to fusing with outmoded scripts that your mind uses to evaluate current and future possibilities. For example, imagine that you've always had a hard time meeting new people. In the past when introduced to new people, you felt uncomfortable and awkward. It always took a long time for you to feel relaxed enough to initiate conversation and share information. Your personal script regarding meeting new people is full of thoughts such as *I hate meeting new people, I feel so awkward at parties where I don't know anyone,* or *I always feel that people are staring at me.* These thoughts and feelings make it difficult for you to join groups or clubs and meet new people. Because of your discomfort, you avoid doing things you'd really like to do, such as learning how to play tennis and bridge. You think you'd really enjoy these activities, but the thought of taking lessons and joining a club make you uncomfortable. Rather than accept the initial discomfort and take steps to do these things, you decide against it and stay stuck in your comfort zone. When this happens, you fear the worst rather than anticipate the best possible outcome associated with trying something new.

The following activity, My Personal Scrapbook, focuses on examining your outdated scripts and how they contribute to your avoidance of potentially enriching new experiences.

ASSESSMENT ACTIVITY:
My Personal Scrapbook

INSTRUCTIONS

1. Divide your life into segments (infancy, early childhood, teen years, and so on) and write these categories down across the top of individual sheets of scrapbook paper.

2. For each segment, gather a couple of photographs of yourself or stories about you. Include ones that bring back both pleasant and painful memories. (If you don't have pictures, newspaper clippings, and so on handy, make this a two-part activity. For part 1, gather the material. Part 2 will incorporate the remainder of the instructions.)

3. Mount each picture or clipping on a larger sheet of paper—use a separate piece of paper for each item—leaving two or three inches of space for you to write something about it.

4. For each item, describe the things about you displayed in the item that still hold true (you still like to play basketball, ride a horse, and so on).

5. For each item, describe the things about you displayed in the item that are no longer true.

6. Ask yourself which of the things in #5 that are no longer true contribute to your current stress and avoidance of new experiences.

7. Take any individual sheet that contains an image or description of you that's outdated and contributes to your stress and avoidance. Put that sheet on a table and, keeping your eyes on it, step three feet away from it.

8. Repeat step #7, but now step six feet away. Tell yourself, *I can distance myself from these outdated images and scripts of myself that create stress and hold me back. While these are part of me, I'm much more than the sum total of these outdated pictures and stories from the past.*

You can incorporate what you've just done in this activity into your life as a whole. In time, you can learn to step back and view the content of your self more objectively and not let outmoded scripts and images keep you from taking on new challenges and moving forward in your life.

Lack of Clarity Concerning Values

A *value* is a combination of a concept, a belief system, and a pattern of behavior that you hold in the highest regard possible. Unlike thoughts or beliefs, which are quite malleable and can be changed by acquiring new information and empirical evidence, your values are much harder to change. Some of the things you value exist independently of empirical evidence.

Take honesty as an example. Honesty as a concept really revolves around being truthful in specific circumstances. Being truthful involves a system of beliefs regarding how you should behave in a variety of situations to demonstrate this. A pattern of honest behavior consists of your actions— what you actually *do*—to demonstrate your truthfulness under a variety of circumstances. Steve, for example, values honesty. Yesterday he found a wallet containing several hundred dollars in cash as well as credit cards and a driver's license. Steve could have easily pocketed the money and thrown the wallet away or returned it without the cash, and no one, except him, would have known what happened. Instead of doing either, he called the owner and returned the wallet and its contents. He even refused a reward, telling the shocked owner, "I wouldn't feel comfortable taking a reward for doing what I think is the right thing and being honest." Steve's actions (returning the wallet and refusing the reward) were consistent with his beliefs about how an honest person would behave in such a circumstance.

In order to live out your values as Steve did, you must know what your values are. *Values clarification* is the process of identifying, accepting, and acting on your values. It involves four steps: (1) exploring, (2) choosing and ranking, (3) publicly affirming, and (4) acting. We'll go over these in detail in chapter 4, but for now, I'll make a few general comments. Most people never take the time to clarify their own values. They live their lives according to the values and goals set for them by others, such as their family, spouse, or culture. They never question whether or not these values work for them. If you live your life according to what other people value rather than what you value, you're going to have a more stressful life, since this will ultimately cause a lot of conflict. When you're not clear about your values, you're like a sailboat without a rudder. The direction of your life and your behavior at any given moment are subject to the prevailing winds (or peer pressure, societal expectations, and so on). Think of your values as the rudder that steers the ship called your life as it sails toward the goals you've set for it.

Inaction, Impulsivity, and Rigidity

Inaction, impulsivity, and rigidity are closely related to the other five components of psychological inflexibility. In particular, they're closely related to a lack of clear values. Inaction is often due to a lack of clarity of values and goal setting. If you're unclear about what you value in life and have no specific goals, it's easy to get stuck and do nothing. Inaction, or taking no action, is the opposite of taking responsibility for your life and behaving in ways that are consistent with your values.

Acting impulsively is also related to a lack of values. When you're unclear about your direction in life because your values and goals are unclear, you often jump at trying anything that sounds good without really thinking through how your actions will impact your long-term well-being. Being impulsive is often a by-product of the happiness trap. Our culture perpetuates the myth that unhappiness or feeling bad means there's something wrong with you. As a result, people in America spend billions of dollars on drugs, toys, and advice to avoid feeling bad at all costs. Temporary relief from pain becomes the goal of life instead of long-term planning and acceptance of discomfort and setbacks. When this is the case, it's easy to run from one quick fix to another in an impulsive quest for happiness.

Rigidity, as we've already mentioned, is the polar opposite of flexibility. Being rigid is an ineffective way to try to protect yourself from unhappiness. Being rigid keeps you in your comfort zone because it keeps you in a familiar thinking and behaving pattern. When you're rigid, you try to avoid or control the painful thoughts, emotions, and behaviors that often accompany taking *valued action* (behaving in ways that are consistent with your values and goals).

WILLINGNESS TO TAKE ACTION

ACT incorporates *willingness training* to help you break through your inactivity, rigidity, and avoidance and take valued action. A key component of meeting your goals and living a life that's consistent with what you value is being willing to take action. Willingness is based on trust, faith, and giving up trying to control, eliminate, or avoid your pain and suffering. Willingness involves trusting that you can take action despite your troubling thoughts and painful emotions, and that you can not only reach your goals but emerge from the process in a better position to manage them in the future. ACT frequently uses metaphors to teach willingness and other skills. Metaphors can help you understand the underlying ACT concepts and theories without having to wade through technical psychological jargon. The following exercise, adapted from the classic ACT metaphor Monsters on the Bus (Luoma, Hayes, and Walser 2007), illustrates this concept of learning to do what matters to you despite your own stressful thoughts and emotions.

DEFUSION AND WILLINGNESS ACTIVITY: The Bus

Think of yourself as a bus driver. Every day you have a route to drive. As you drive the bus along your route each day, you pick up various passengers. Some of these passengers are new, some are regulars, some are friendly, some are nasty, and some are troublesome. As your passengers get on the bus, you keep an eye on them, pay more attention to some than others, but you realize that you can't keep them from getting on the bus. All you can do is observe them and keep an eye out for trouble. Throughout the day, these different types of passengers get on and off your bus. In time, all of the passengers get off the bus, and you finish your route and park the bus in the garage for the night.

Now think of this bus route as a list of your goals for the day. Each goal represents something you want or need to do to live a life according to your values. Instead of passengers getting on and off the bus, imagine them to be the stressful thoughts, personal scripts, mental images, and painful emotions that stand in the way of your meeting your goals for the day. As you did with the passengers on the bus, you can step back and observe these thoughts, scripts, images, and emotions, and accept the fact that they threaten you and you don't know how to cope with them. As you did with the passengers on the bus, you accept that they'll also come and go and you can continue to drive your bus while coexisting with your passengers. You realize that each day brings a new dawn, a new route, and a new set of passengers on the journey of your life.

Enjoy the journey!

&

Taking valued action, while coexisting with your stressful thoughts and emotions, is a skill that you can develop with practice. In this book, you'll learn that you can't control, avoid, or eliminate 100 percent of your stressors. As with the passengers on the bus, sometimes the best way to manage your stressors is to coexist with them and let them come and go as you meet the goals you set out to accomplish.

CHAPTER 3

Controlling, Eliminating, and Managing Stress

Most people fail in their attempts at stress management because they confuse managing stress with eliminating or controlling it. By definition, "eliminate" means to cause something to disappear or to permanently get rid of something. There are many things in your life you can eliminate. If you don't like your job, you can quit and find a new one. If you don't like the color of your house, you can paint it a new color. If you don't like your car, you can get rid of it and buy a new one. But stress doesn't work quite like that.

WHY YOU CAN'T CONTROL OR ELIMINATE 100 PERCENT OF YOUR STRESS

Unfortunately you can't eliminate all of your stress because stress is a part of life. You might be able to eliminate one or two sources of stress (such as that stressful job and annoying car), but you soon find that they're quickly replaced with other sources of stress. Even when you're sleeping, your body is exposed to environmental stressors, such as changes in room temperature, that force you to do things such as shiver in order to stay warm. The only time you are really "stress-free" is when you're dead and your physical body ceases to function.

When you "control" something, you regulate it. Think about controlling the amount of hot water in your shower. You turn the water on and adjust the mixture of hot and cold water to control the temperature. When it's just right, you step in the shower and start to lather up. Unfortunately you don't have "hot" and "cold" stress faucets to turn on and off at your discretion. Fortunately you don't need to control stress in order to manage it. Let's see how ACT deals with the issue of controlling stress.

ACT provides a unique perspective on trying to control or eliminate stress. As you've seen in chapters 1 and 2, stress occurs when you feel that the threat, harm, or loss posed by a potential stressor is greater than your ability to cope with it. If you're like most people, you probably try to deal with potential stressors by trying to control or eliminate them. This strategy, according to ACT, is doomed to fail at least 50 percent of the time. Why? Because it's estimated that 50 percent of stress is caused by your thoughts, personal scripts, mental images, and emotions. Throughout the rest of the book, I'll refer to these sources as your *internal potential stressors*.

Internal potential stressors, as you'll see in this chapter, are beyond your ability to control. This leaves you with trying to manage stress as your only reasonable goal. When you "manage" something, you handle or cope with it. When you manage something, you realize you have limited control over it and you accept that. For example, if you decided to manage your child's baseball team, you realize that, while there are things you can do to manage the squad (organize practices, set up travel plans, and have contingencies for everything from bad weather to canceled games), you can do very little to control the outcome of any game. You realize that some players are less motivated, talented, and interested than others. You accept that games will be cancelled for inclement weather, inability to field enough players, summer vacations, and a host of other reasons. You also accept the fact that baseball is a game, and inherent in all games is the element of luck (a lucky hit, an unlucky called third strike, a timely error by the other team, and so on). Despite these elements that make it impossible to control the outcome of the season or eliminate all of the things that might hinder your team's success, you still agree to manage the squad. In essence when you do this, you also agree to accept what you can't control or eliminate. Managing your stress works the same way.

A LOOK AT INTERNAL POTENTIAL STRESSORS

As I described in chapter 2, your brain is a 24/7 thinking-and-feeling machine that constantly processes information and is capable of running multiple programs at the same time. These programs are your thoughts, personal scripts, mental images, and emotions. While thoughts, scripts, images, and emotions are similar in that they're capable of creating stress, they're different enough to warrant discussing them separately.

Thoughts

Thoughts are the basic building blocks of your cognitive functioning—that is, how and what you think. Your thoughts are related to a host of things including, but not limited to, your IQ, health status, life experience, body chemistry, and emotional state. Some of your thoughts are based on empirical evidence and facts, while others are not. Some of your thoughts are rational and logical, while others couldn't be more irrational or illogical. Some of your thoughts spring out of emotions you're feeling or mental images you're focusing on, while others do not. Some of your thoughts originate from your conscious effort to create them, while others just come and go like the wind.

Personal Scripts

Your thoughts combine to form personal scripts about specific aspects of your life and your personality. As we discussed in chapter 2, your *personal scripts* are the little story lines that you've created for all of the experiences you've had in the past, are living in the present, and imagine will occur in the future. You have personal scripts about your childhood, work, school, relationships, politics, and the world at large. Like your thoughts, these scripts can be logical or illogical, factual or inaccurate, neutral or emotionally charged, and real or imagined. Many of these scripts are outdated and based on your past failures and painful emotions. You carry these around in your brain, and they often interfere with your ability to enjoy the present moment and take valued action.

Mental Images

Mental images are the internal pictures you see when you close your eyes and observe your thoughts and personal scripts. Mental images can be neutral or linked to emotions. Some of your mental images are accompanied by pleasant emotions like hope, love, and satisfaction, while others are linked to painful or negative emotions like jealousy, fear, worry, and anxiety. In his book *The Happiness Trap*, psychotherapist Russ Harris (2007) calls these latter types of mental images "scary pictures" because when you "see" them inside your head, you take them so literally that they scare you as much as if they were actually happening to you in person instead of just existing in your mind.

Emotions

Emotions are essentially impulses to act. They're the result of an evolutionary process that forces us to stop, pay attention, analyze the threat associated with a situation, and act, all within a split second. Daniel Goleman (1997), in his groundbreaking book *Emotional Intelligence*, points out that the root of the word "emotion" is from the Latin *motere,* meaning to move; the prefix "e" added to the root means to "move away." Some of your stronger emotions like fear and anger are linked to your perception of threat and the mobilization of energy that occurs during the fight-or-flight response. Often if you're afraid or angry, you'll feel threatened and susceptible to stress.

THE RELATIONSHIP OF INTERNAL POTENTIAL STRESSORS TO STRESS

Your thoughts, personal scripts, mental images, and emotions are related to both parts of the stress appraisal model we discussed in chapter 1, including (1) the threat, harm, or loss you associate with them, and (2) your perceived ability to cope with them. For example, your mind can churn out thoughts, personal scripts, mental images, and emotions that you perceive as threatening or having the ability to cause you harm or loss. Whether this is factual or not doesn't matter. If you view them as threatening or able to cause harm or loss, they can trigger a stress response. These same internal potential stressors play a part in your perceived ability to cope. If you think you can cope with them, you probably won't be stressed. If you think you can't cope with them, you probably will be stressed.

Because your brain works 24/7 processing thoughts, personal scripts, mental images, and emotions, it has the ability to conjure up just about every conceivable thing that might go wrong with a situation therefore it can create fear and worry about outcomes you can't possibly predict, control, or eliminate. Trying to control this 24/7 process sometimes feels like trying to stop a runaway train. Rather than trying to eliminate or control your runaway train/brain, it's often better to just step out of its way and watch it pass by. (See the Train Watching defusion activity later in this chapter.)

As we discussed in chapter 2, your mind also has the ability to link different past frames of reference to help you solve current and future problems. This ability to synthesize past and present information and project it into the future is a distinctly human trait that gives you a tremendous advantage over other mammals. It allows you to use planning and problem solving to avoid, control, and eliminate problems in your life.

Unfortunately this same ability works exactly the opposite way when you try to control your internal stressors. While you can control, avoid, and eliminate external potential stressors related to your behavior and your environment (use of drugs, choice of job, and so on), the harder you try to do the same with your internal stressors, the more intense they become. As I discussed in chapter 2, ACT research has demonstrated that the more you focus on your internal stressors and try to "work on" them, the worse they get. This almost seems counterintuitive. It certainly goes against the grain of most forms of Western psychotherapy that advocate that you should "work on" your emotional problems and try to gain "insight" into why you think and feel the way you do.

Instead of trying to control negative emotions and work on eliminating them, ACT research had found that a better strategy is to just accept them for what they are, coexist with them, and get on with doing the things you need and want to do in your life. This shouldn't be confused with denying the existence of the problem or the emotions and thoughts associated with it. In fact, ACT teaches mindfulness and willingness in order to help you learn how to observe and accept the thoughts and emotions without being drawn into an automatic response. In other words, learning how to take valued action, while coexisting with these negative thoughts and painful emotions, is the best way to deal with them.

Taking valued action, while coexisting with your negative thoughts and painful emotions is a skill that you can develop. It just takes some practice. A good place to start is understanding some of the common thinking and feeling traps most people fall into when dealing with stressful thoughts, personal scripts, mental images, and emotions.

TEN COMMON STRESSFUL THINKING AND FEELING TRAPS

When you're stressed, you usually get caught in one of what I refer to as the "ten common stressful thinking and feeling traps." I'll briefly discuss what these traps are in this section. We'll talk about how to get out of these traps later in the book.

The "Thoughts Are Reality" Trap

In *The Happiness Trap*, Russ Harris (2007) describes the thinking myths that are often related to stress. The "thoughts are reality" trap is based on the perception that the thoughts you have about something represent the objective reality of the situation. In fact, your thoughts are just part of your conceptualized self unless you're experiencing them firsthand in the present moment. You fall into the trap when you think they're the actual event instead of just your thoughts about it.

An example of this is reading about something that was reported in the newspaper. You read the story, get the facts, and create your own mental image of the story and your own thoughts about it. Your reality of the story is really your version of it as it passes through the filter of your conceptualized self. Your thoughts about the event are really based on secondhand information and your own interpretation of those secondhand facts.

The "Thoughts Are True" Trap

The "thoughts are true" trap is based on the belief that just because you think of something, the thoughts must be true. Many of the thoughts you have are really opinions or evaluations. For example, imagine you're walking to work and you find yourself thinking about something a politician said that's related to increasing foreign aid to a country in Eastern Europe. You don't even know where the country is or what the increased foreign aid is supposed to accomplish, but you say to yourself, *What a stupid idea, those people don't need the help. They'll just waste the money.* In fact, there's no truth to this belief; it was just a random thought that crossed your mind, one of many that morning. You have no evidence to support your belief that the country will waste the money. You believe the statement merely because your mind created it. Not only do you believe it, it makes you stressed because you find your mind continually returning to the thought that the country will just "waste the money."

Your brain constantly offers up opinions and evaluations on everything. These thoughts are neither true nor false, they merely *are*. You've probably found that some people (perhaps even you) love to argue over these types of thoughts and can get pretty stressed out trying to convince others of their "truth," when in fact they're merely personal judgments and opinions. You fall into the "thoughts are true" trap when you fail to realize that these truths are really your personal judgments or opinions.

The "All Thoughts Are Equally Important" Trap

The "all thoughts are equally important" trap gives equal weight to all of your thoughts. As you've seen so far, some of your thoughts just represent your opinion, judgment, or evaluation of something. Some of your thoughts are very important, like those associated with major decisions in your life related to work, relationships, citizenship, and so on. Others are not very important at all and may not even be connected to your day-to-day existence. For example, imagine that you've just finished reading the newspaper. In the first section, you've read distressing articles about the air quality in Beijing, China; the slumping U.S. stock market; a dead whale found on the beaches in the Outer Banks of North Carolina; and the increased price of airfare for the coming holiday weekend. You find yourself thinking, *It's really horrible about the air in China—those people are ruining the air for everyone. Oh my God, our economy will never recover. Those poor whales, they're always turning up dead on our shores; we're probably killing them all with our pollution. Those airlines should be ashamed about what they charge; people will never be able to fly anywhere.* Not only are most of these thoughts illogical because they exaggerate and generalize the facts, most of them don't directly apply to you or affect your day-to-day life. In fact, the only one that directly applies to you, a stockholder living in the Midwest, is the slumping U.S. stock market. The other thoughts are not as important as this one, and giving them equal weight can add to your stress. For any of the unimportant thoughts, it's perfectly okay to say to yourself, *This thought isn't really worth paying too much attention to.* You fall into the "all thoughts are equally important" trap when you take all of your thoughts too seriously and assign them the same high importance.

The "Thoughts Are Orders" Trap

The "thoughts are orders" trap revolves around the belief that just because you think something, you have to act on it. Since not all thoughts are equal, and some are pretty silly or potentially embarrassing, it really is okay to say to yourself, *My mind is ordering me around again.* You don't have to act on all of your thoughts. This is especially true if your mind is ordering you to buy into other people's universal stressors. For example, imagine you were just exposed to something that almost universally stresses out 99 percent of my students and clients who drive—that is, being cut off by a reckless driver. Imagine that as soon as you get cut off, your mind tells you, *What a jerk that guy is for doing this to me. I'll show him—I'll catch up to him and cut him off and drop my speed 15 mph.* As soon as you think this thought, you interpret it as marching orders to change your normal, safe driving behavior and cut the other driver off. On top of this, you find yourself getting tense and angry as your thoughts trigger a stress response. You don't have to follow your mind's orders. You can simply view those thoughts for what they are—"crazy thoughts." You fall into the "thoughts are orders trap" when you mindlessly act in response to unhelpful thoughts.

The "Thoughts Are Threats" Trap

My favorite thinking trap is the "thoughts are threats" trap. I'm sorry to be redundant but thoughts are *thoughts*, nothing more and nothing less. One of the most profound messages I received in my childhood was "Sticks and stones will break my bones, but words will never hurt me." Unless you allow them to, thoughts (like words) can't harm you. Thinking that something can harm you is different from actually *being* in harm's way. For example, you might read a story about the economy and the current mortgage mess and devaluation of the housing market, and it might really stress you out. You might feel threatened by the economic and housing events occurring around the country and feel unable to cope with them.

As soon as you connect those two variables, feeling threatened and feeling unable to cope with the situation, you get stressed. In fact, however, you have a very secure job, own a home in a neighborhood where property values actually rose, and are doing quite well financially. The thoughts you have about the problems in the housing and mortgage markets are just your thoughts; they're not the reality of your life at this moment. You fall into the "thoughts are threats" trap when you automatically project things that are threatening to others onto yourself.

The "Old, Outdated Thoughts and Scripts" Trap

As I discussed in chapter 2, everyone carries around outdated thoughts and personal scripts about themselves. In many cases, these are accompanied by outdated mental images. Like outdated photographs of how you looked twenty years ago, they've contributed to who you are, but they're often just faded representations of your past. In many cases, these faded snapshots, thoughts, and scripts are no longer based on the reality of who you currently are. Lying just below the surface like land mines ready to explode when you step on them, these outdated images, thoughts, and scripts can sabotage your best efforts to manage stress and grow. When you buy into these unhelpful thoughts and personal scripts, they undermine your self-confidence and block you from taking the valued action you so desperately want and need.

The "Scary Pictures Are Real" Trap

As I mentioned earlier, Russ Harris (2007) refers to stressful or frightening mental images as "scary pictures." Equating the scary pictures in your mind to reality is like going to a horror movie and actually believing that the crazed killer with the chainsaw just cut the innocent victim's head off. Scary pictures in your mind are just that—pictures in your mind. They don't exist in the real world in the present moment, and they don't pose an actual physical threat to your well-being. They're like the crazy thoughts and scripts that your very creative mind churns out nonstop all day long. Sometimes these scary pictures can create stress, especially when they conjure up threatening scenarios that you feel unable to cope with. For example, imagine that you have a job interview tomorrow for a position that pays better, offers greater benefits than your current one, and is closer to home. As you close your eyes and think about the interview, you see yourself sitting across from the interviewer and drawing a blank in response to a question he asked you. You "watch" yourself turn beet red, break out into a cold sweat, and mumble some incoherent answer that dooms the outcome of the interview. In fact, none of this has actually happened, yet the scary picture of tomorrow's interview created in your mind has triggered a stress response. Instead of equating your scary pictures with reality, you could just as easily tell yourself, *There goes the old movie projector again*, and then view them as merely another crazy picture show.

The "Permanence" Trap

Martin Seligman (1990), a pioneer in the positive psychology movement, believes that each of us has what he calls an "explanatory style" that's related to the way we perceive potential stressors. Our *explanatory style* has three key components that relate to stressful thinking: permanence, pervasiveness, and personalization. *Permanence* refers to how long you believe stressful events will last. If you view a potentially stressful situation as something that will "last forever" and affect you permanently, you're falling into the "permanence" trap. Very few stressors last forever. Some major life events such as the death of a loved one are permanent, but the stressful effects of experiencing them do not have to be. Remember, the stressor is kept active by your thoughts related to the loss and your inability to cope with it. Suffering a catastrophic loss doesn't have to last forever. If you allow yourself to grieve, seek help, and move forward in your life, even major life events do not have to be permanently stressful.

People who view temporary setbacks and stressors as permanently affecting their lives tend to be more pessimistic, another trait that Seligman found to be associated with increased stress. Someone who is overly pessimistic uses words such as "always" and "never" to describe the permanence of potential stressors. If you find yourself saying things like *These kinds of things always happen to me,* or *I'll never be able to get it right,* or *I'll never get out of debt,* or *I'll never find someone to love me,* then you've fallen into the "permanence" trap and need to get out of it.

Someone who is more optimistic tends to view stressful events and situations as temporary, and they'll say things to themselves like *Although this is a very painful thing to go through, it too will pass,* or *I'm really upset over this, but I'll get over it in a couple of days.* People who are more optimistic can even admit to feeling temporarily overwhelmed and unable to cope. The difference is that people who are more optimistic believe that stressful situations and the feelings that accompany them are temporary and do not represent a permanent state of being. You fall into the "permanence" trap when you get stuck by fusing with ideas like "always" and "never." When this happens, you lose your faith in the future. You no longer act on your values and live the life you want to lead.

The "Pervasiveness" Trap

The second of Seligman's three P's, *pervasiveness,* relates to the extent of the influence of a stressor or stressful situation. People who are more pessimistic tend to view the effects of potential stressors as pervasive, or affecting every aspect of their lives. People who are more optimistic tend to view stressors as context specific and not affecting every facet of their lives. If you tell yourself things like *I can't do anything right, My whole life sucks,* or *Nothing I do is ever good enough for her,* you've fallen into the "pervasiveness" trap. This kind of thinking is illogical and stressful because it generalizes the results of one facet of your life to all facets of your life.

For instance, someone who is overly pessimistic might view not getting a specific promotion as a measure of their lack of intelligence and ability and believe that they'll never get promoted or succeed at any aspect of their job. They might tell themselves things such as *I am totally stupid and don't deserve to ever get promoted,* or *I'm probably going to wind up losing this job because I can't do anything right,* or *I'll never be able to learn any of the new parts of this job.*

Someone who is more optimistic would view not getting promoted as something specifically related to that particular position at that specific point in their work history. They wouldn't universally associate it with all promotions over their entire association with the company. They'd use the following self-talk to explain the lost promotion: *Boy, that promotion must have been very competitive and I'll have to work harder to get the next one* or *I guess I really haven't proven myself yet and I'll have to see what I can do to position myself for the next promotion that comes up.* You fall into the "pervasiveness" trap when you believe a stressful situation cuts across every aspect of your life, not just the one it's related to.

The "Personalization" Trap

The last of Seligman's three P's, *personalization,* refers to whether you have an "internal" or "external" view of being responsible for your stress. People who are more pessimistic tend to have an *external view of personal responsibility for stress*: they blame others or society for their problems and stress. People who are more optimistic tend to have an *internal view of personal responsibility for stress*: they take personal responsibility for turning potential stressors into actual stressors. Someone who is overly pessimistic would engage in the following kinds of personalization self-talk: *She really made me feel bad* or *Everybody is always making me do things that I don't want to do and getting me all stressed out.* Someone who is more optimistic would probably react in the following way to these situations: *I really feel bad when she acts that way* or *I need to start saying no to things that I really don't want to do and that I find stressful.*

It's important to realize that even the most optimistic person feels pessimistic at times. The difference is that people who are more optimistic bounce back from defeats and weather them better than people who are overly pessimistic. You fall into the "personalization" trap when you blame others for your stress instead of taking personal responsibility for your stressful thinking and inability to cope.

The following tool, My Personal Stressor Journal, will help you start to keep track of the things you find stressful and your perceived ability to cope with them.

ASSESSMENT ACTIVITY:
My Personal Stressor Journal

Starting today, keep a journal of your personal stressors. You can keep this in whatever format you desire: electronic, lined paper, bound journal, or something else. Fill in the categories whenever it's convenient for you: as they occur, at the end of the day, and so on. I recommend that you don't let more than a day pass before recording a stressor. This will keep the details of it from blurring.

Use the following format to log each stressor:

Date:

Potential stressor (be as specific as possible):

Intensity of the potential stressor (1 = lowest, 10 = highest):

Threat, harm, loss associated with it (What was threatening? What did you lose? How were you harmed?):

Thinking/feeling trap (Which trap did you fall into?):

Coping ability (On a scale of 1–10, what did you tell yourself about your ability to cope with this potential stressor? 1 = I can't cope at all, 10 = I can cope completely):

Coping success (Was your coping successful?):

EXAMPLE:

Date: 12/21/08

Potential stressor: Going Christmas shopping at the mall.

Intensity of the potential stressor: 9

Threat, harm, loss associated with it: I hate crowds; they can trigger a panic attack.

Thinking/feeling trap: I fell into the "permanence" trap because I told myself that I'd never be able to handle going Christmas shopping if I didn't avoid the crowds.

Coping ability: 8—I got to the mall early to avoid the crowds.

Coping success: Did not work, mall crowded before it even opened. I had a panic attack while looking for parking.

Throughout the rest of this book, you'll learn how to apply ACT to both assessing the threat, harm, or loss posed by potential stressors and coping with them. In time, this will help you reprogram your brain regarding stressors and your ability to cope with them. You'll find the journal a helpful tool for going back and looking at your personal stressors when learning ACT principles and practices. The more information you accumulate in your journal about your stressors, the easier it will be to learn to assess your stressors and cope with them.

DEFUSING FROM TEN COMMON STRESSFUL THINKING AND FEELING TRAPS

It's futile to fight the thinking and feeling traps or other painful thoughts and emotions. Rather than work against your runaway train/brain, why not either hop on board or simply step out of its way and watch your thoughts and feelings from a safer distance? Once you view your brain as this fascinating 24/7 thinking and feeling machine capable of cranking out thoughts and emotions nonstop, you begin to accept it for what it is and what it does. Acceptance is a big part of ACTing to manage your stress. Accepting that your brain will often tell you things that aren't necessarily true or in your best interest sets the stage for learning how to defuse from them. The following two activities, Train Watching and The Roller Coaster, will help you defuse from the ten common thinking and feeling traps and other painful thoughts and emotions.

DEFUSION ACTIVITY: Train Watching

Imagine that you're on your way home from work and you're approaching a railroad crossing a few miles from home. As you near the crossing, the lights start flashing, bells start clanging, and a barrier descends, warning you of an approaching train and imminent danger. You stop and wait for the train to appear. In a matter of moments, a freight train begins to pass. The train, pulled by a massive locomotive, has what seems to be an endless array of colorful cars and cargo. As you wait for the train to pass, you marvel at such a feat of technology and think about the goods being shipped to people all across the country and in your own neighborhood. You also think about how grateful you are for railroad crossings, because without them, coexisting with freight trains would be very difficult.

Now imagine that same situation, but the railroad crossing is you (the entire you—mind, body, and spirit) and the train is your brain. Imagine that the flashing lights, clanging bells, and descending barrier of the railroad crossing are the warning signs your mind sends you when you're confronted by a potential stressor. You stop, take notice, and feel protected by your mind's own personal crossing.

Imagine the train passes you, and each car represents a stressful thought, personal script, scary picture, or painful emotion. Rather than view these things as something you can control, you see them as passing thoughts, scripts, images, and feelings, all as fleeting as the cars that make up the train. Continue to watch your train roar by, secure in the knowledge that it eventually will pass, the blinking lights and clanging bells going off in your mind will cease, and your personal barrier will rise, allowing you to continue on home to a productive evening.

With practice, you can use this and other defusion activities throughout the book to distance yourself from your stressful thoughts, personal scripts, scary pictures, and painful emotions. The next activity, The Roller Coaster, works slightly differently. But, like Train Watching, it will help you defuse from the ten common thinking and feeling traps and other painful thoughts and emotions. Rather than distance yourself from your stressful thoughts, personal scripts, scary pictures, and painful emotions, it encourages you to hop on board for a wild ride on your emotional roller coaster.

DEFUSION ACTIVITY: The Roller Coaster

Imagine you're in an amusement park with a classic white wooden roller coaster. You approach the roller coaster and feel its power. As you stand next to the coaster, you have mixed feelings about riding it. Your mind tells you how thrilling it'll be and how frightened it'll make you. You remember your past experiences on the ride and chills run up and down your spine. Throwing caution to the wind, you buy a ticket and take a seat. Over the next few minutes, you hang on for dear life as the roller coaster rises to the top of its highest point and then plunges you through a series of death-defying twists and turns, ultimately depositing you in one piece back at the boarding platform. As you get off the ride, legs wobbling, you walk down the ramp past all of the people who stand there, mouths open, in awe of your courage (or craziness). You smile inwardly for having the nerve to take the ride of your lifetime.

Now imagine the roller coaster is a potential stressor, something that you really want to confront, but it's very daunting and challenging. As you approach the coaster, you feel the power of this challenge, and the lure of the reward at the end of the ride urges you on. As the protective bar is lowered and you're safely secured in your seat, the stressful thoughts, personal scripts, mental images, and emotions you have regarding what you're about to undertake begin to kick in. As you begin your challenging task, your roller-coaster ride begins, and as you're pulled to the apex of the ride, your anticipation of what's to follow reaches its peak. As you continue to work on your challenging task, you plunge through a series of death-defying emotional twists and turns. Your thoughts get pushed and pulled in many different directions. You conjure up a thousand different scary pictures as you are thrust into one seemingly death-defying blind turn after another. Your stomach churns, and you fight the bile rising up in your throat because you know you can survive this ride and it's almost over. As you finish your challenging task and your ride ends, you feel a little wobbly and worn out from the adrenaline rush of your wild but productive ride. You smile inwardly for having the nerve to take the ride of your lifetime.

As you can see, the Roller Coaster activity is not for the faint-hearted. In it, I'm asking you to be willing to experience all of the painful thoughts and emotions that accompany the challenging task you'd like to complete. Meeting challenging goals and completing difficult tasks often means that you must be willing to accept the pain and suffering that goes along with them. The Roller Coaster activity can help you defuse some of the stress associated with this if you're willing to accept the painful thoughts and emotions that accompany the challenging task you'd like to complete.

CONTROLLING SOME STRESSORS, SOME OF THE TIME

As you've already learned, your internal potential stressors are your stressful thoughts, personal scripts, mental images, and painful emotions. These internal phenomena exist in your mind, come and go as they please, and are beyond your ability to control. What you do have a great deal of control over, however, are different aspects of your external physical environment and your behavior. I'll refer to these as your *external potential stressors*. Let's start with a quick examination of your physical environment.

Your Macro- and Microenvironments

Your physical environment can be broken down into two different dimensions, your "microenvironment" and your "macroenvironment." Your *microenvironment* includes the people and things in your immediate environment that you interact with every day. It includes your school, home, work site, neighborhood, family, friends, and associates. Your social support system is also part of your microenvironment. Your microenvironment greatly affects your health and personal safety as well as your stress. It influences whether you are at risk for and fear such things as theft, crime, and violence. Air and water quality, noise pollution, overcrowding, traffic, and other factors that influence your stress levels can also be part of your microenvironment.

What all of these aspects of your microenvironment have in common is that you can exert some degree of control over them if you find that they contribute to your stress. For example, you can change jobs if your current one is stressful or unfulfilling. While changing jobs isn't easy, you could do it if you developed a comprehensive job search plan and gave yourself enough time to implement it.

The same could be said for changing other aspects of your microenvironment, such as your relationships. If you found that you were bored or disenchanted with some of your current friends and associates, you could take action to meet new people. You could join groups, take classes, or volunteer your time to support a cause or organization you believe in. In the course of doing this, you could meet new people and make some new friends.

Your *macroenvironment* is much harder to control. Events occurring in your state, the country, and the world-at-large offer fewer opportunities to control. Many people are frustrated and stressed by this. They feel powerless and unable to make a difference in events that go on beyond their microenvironments. Others get involved in organizations that span state, national, and international borders and do whatever they can to make their voice heard and influence the way these organizations function. Other people run for political office and try to make a difference.

Throughout the rest of the book, we'll examine different aspects of your micro- and macroenvironments to see how they contribute to your stress and how you can manage this. We'll discuss many different techniques that you can use to abolish, avoid, or alter your environmental stressors.

Your Behavior: Taking Valued Action

The second thing you can control regarding your stress is your behavior. ACT folks like to refer to *behavior* as taking valued action—in other words, your behavior acts in harmony with your values or doing what needs to be done to reach your goals. Your behavior relates to stress in two ways: it can be a source of stress or a valuable tool in managing it.

Let's use procrastination as an example of stress-producing behavior. Procrastination is a behavior, one in which you put off doing what needs to be done. Sometimes you put things off to the last minute and then get stressed as you rush to finish as the deadline draws near. In this example, your behavior actually became a stressor. Had you paced yourself and worked consistently to finish the task, you could have minimized feeling threatened by and unable to cope with the work. In essence, by controlling your behavior you could have prevented the task from becoming stressful.

Let's use meditation as an example of stress-reducing behavior. There's a lot of evidence showing that meditation works in reducing stress. Basically meditation teaches you how to slow down and relax your body by becoming more mindful of what's going on in the present moment. If you practice meditation faithfully for three to six months, you should begin to notice changes in the way you view yourself and your potential stressors. Getting to this point, however, requires daily practice. Putting time aside to practice and following through by practicing in a meaningful way are behaviors that you can control.

෴

Throughout the remainder of this book, we'll explore many behavioral strategies for managing stress. All of them require a commitment to set time aside to think about them and to practice on a regular basis. But by making this commitment, you'll reap the benefits of a new—and healthier—relationship with your stress.

CHAPTER 4

Values and Stress

Your values mirror your personality and are central to defining who you are as a person. While your knowledge, attitudes, and beliefs strongly contribute to who you are, they're more amenable to change. Your values represent the ideals you cherish most, the ones you hold most dear and are least willing (or able) to change. Many of your personal scripts revolve around your values and become the bedrock of your self.

When you were a child, your values mirrored those of your parents. As you moved through childhood and adolescence and into young adulthood, your values began to shift and more accurately represented what you truly believed in and stood for. Most of the time you didn't even realize that this shift had occurred until you had a *values conflict,* that is, when one of your values clashed with a value held by someone else (such as a parent, spouse, or employer). Values conflicts are among the most threatening of all internal potential stressors because they represent a threat to what you cherish most in life. When something is a threat to your values, it rocks you to your core because it threatens the very foundation of your personality.

VALUES CLARIFICATION: A FOUR-PART PROCESS

Values clarification is a process of helping you clarify and stand up for what you truly value. You can clarify your values at any point in your life. Sometimes the process makes you realize that the values you've held for a long time no longer work for you or represent who you are as a person. At other times, the process reaffirms for you the things you hold most dear.

If you're serious about ACTing to manage your stress, you need to clarify your values because they're intimately related to your goals and the steps you need to take to get where you want and need to be in your life.

There are many different models to use to help you clarify your values. I prefer a variation on the original model developed by Sidney Simon, Leland Howe, and Howard Kirschenbaum (1995). Values clarification is a four-step process: (1) exploring your values, (2) choosing and ranking your values, (3) publicly affirming your values, and (4) acting on your values. Let's take a closer look at each of these steps.

Exploring Your Values

If you're like most of my students and clients, you've probably never formally explored your values. You've probably thought about them from time to time, but never really written them down and thought about how they relate to your personality and your goals. During the first step of the values clarification process, you use a variety of exercises and activities to identify your values about what matters most to you in life.

Choosing and Ranking Your Values

During the second step of the process, you rank your values in terms of the most important to the least important. Your most important values are your *core values*, the ones that are central to who you are and for which you would fight or die. People typically identify such things as their country, spouse, children, religion, and freedom as core values. These are the values that are most likely to create stress when they're threatened. Surrounding your core values are lesser-held values that you hold dear but to which you are not as strongly committed. Values related to things such as political beliefs, cultural traditions, personal attributes such as intelligence and beauty, pursuits such as recreation and sports typically fall into this category, but some of these things might represent core values to you. Don't worry if this is the case; you can choose and rank your values any way you want to. Everyone values things differently. Some people rank things such as politics and economic issues very high while others couldn't care less about these things. Don't worry about how your values match up to other people's. The most important thing is to be true to your own values.

Publicly Affirming Your Values

Don't worry, you don't have to literally stand on a soapbox and proclaim your values to the world. During the third step of values clarification, you simply let others know what you value rather than keeping your values to yourself. This could happen with just one other person in a private conversation or in front of a large group. When you publicly affirm your values, you share them with others through your written and spoken words. This can be very empowering and help you develop the courage to live up to your convictions. Be aware, however, that sharing your values may at times be challenging to others. Therefore, if you're new to sharing your values, share them first with people you know and trust.

Acting on Your Values

The fourth and final step of values clarification involves taking action. Talking about your values is entirely different from acting on them. When you take action, you test the validity of your values. Some people are more verbal than others. They feel comfortable talking about what they value as well as behaving in ways that demonstrate how they feel. Other people prefer to let their actions speak for themselves. What kind of person are you?

CATEGORIZING YOUR VALUES

There are many different ways to categorize your values. Drawing on the various dimensions of health, the values work of Steve Hayes (2005), and my work in stress management for over twenty-five years, I've developed a framework of ten categories that will help give your values clarification some structure. The ten values categories are intimate relationships, family relationships, friendships and other relationships, health, spirituality, finances, learning, work, the environment, and civics. I broke the relationship category into three separate areas because so much stress is associated with different kinds of relationships that it might be helpful to look at them separately. In the next section, I'll briefly describe each of the ten categories of values I've chosen and then give you the opportunity to clarify what you value in these areas.

Intimate Relationships

Your intimate relationships are those that involve any combination of romantic love, sex, and commitment to another person. Intimacy, by definition, implies that the relationship involves a deeper level of sharing personal information and experience than friendships or other more casual relationships. Romantic love, sex, and commitment can be expressed in a variety of ways. You can define these terms for yourself.

Family Relationships

When assessing this category, you can define family any way you want. It could be nuclear (parents and siblings), extended (add in aunts, uncles, cousins, grandparents, and so on), or any other kind of family (mixture of friends, family, domestic partners, and so on) you are a member of. What you value about your relationships with family is strongly influenced by your culture and the way you were raised. Obviously any pattern of neglect or abuse in your family history will strongly influence your present values.

Friendships and Other Relationships

This category covers the entire spectrum from close friends to casual associates. It differs from the other two relationship categories because these relationships aren't among family members and do not include romantic love, sex, or the same type of commitment you would pledge to an intimate partner.

Health

Health can be defined many ways. In 1947, the World Health Organization (WHO 1947) defined health as "a state of complete physical, social, and mental well-being, not merely the absence of disease" (29). Since then, it's been redefined by the wellness movement as a process of moving toward optimal functioning across the physical, social, spiritual, emotional, intellectual, environmental, and occupational dimensions. (For a definition of "wellness," see the website of the National Wellness Institute at nationalwellness.org/index.php?id_tier=2&id_c=25.) This way of defining health views it as existing on a continuum from low-level functioning (ill health) to high-level functioning (optimal). Besides assessing how well your body functions—rather than just looks or feels—it also includes your intellectual and emotional well-being, your spirituality, your social relationships, and your work and other environments. It encompasses every aspect of your health.

Spirituality

Your spirituality revolves around feeling connected to something beyond your self. The sense of feeling connected to something/someone beyond the self is the essence of all definitions of spirituality. One way to express spirituality is through participation in organized religious activities. This usually involves a belief in a supreme being or higher supernatural force, as well as a formalized code of conduct to live by. In a secular sense, spirituality can manifest itself through a connection to something greater than oneself. Whether it's being part of a community, working to save the environment, helping to feed the needy, or committing oneself to world peace, the underlying feeling is one of a perception of life as having meaning beyond the self.

Finances

Your finances cover things such as how much money you want or need to earn, your saving and spending habits, and your budgeting concerns. Your values related to money influence everything from your choice of occupation to your expectations for retirement. Financial concerns are a major source of stress for both individuals and couples. Values conflicts about money are among the top three reasons married couples file for divorce.

Learning

This category relates to both formal and informal ways of acquiring new knowledge, information, and skills. It also covers what you value regarding degrees, qualifications, certifications, licenses, and other formal and informal acknowledgments of your learning. Learning can also relate to what you value about educational institutions (schools, colleges, and so on) and life experience.

Work

Your work values revolve around your job and work environment. Work is an important part of life, offering opportunities for personal growth, earning income, socialization, and making a contribution to society. There are three key components of your work: (1) the physical work environment, (2) social relationships with coworkers and/or bosses, and (3) your actual job. The physical environment of your work site includes such things as temperature, lighting, noise, ventilation, and ergonomic design. Social relationships between you and your coworkers and/or bosses include both on- and off-the-job encounters. Job tasks involve the specific nature of the activities performed, such as writing, teaching, driving, typing, operating machinery, and so on.

The Environment

Your environment serves as the physical context in which all of the rest of your activities play out. As we've discussed previously in this book, your environment can be broken down into the micro and macro levels. Your microenvironment includes your immediate surroundings: school, home, neighborhood, town, city, and so on. This environment greatly affects your stress and the daily quality of your life. Your microenvironment involves factors such as air and water quality, privacy, safety, opportunities for recreation, and others. Your macroenvironment encompasses your state, country, and the world-at-large.

Civics

Civics is a broad category that covers different aspects of citizenship ranging from being a responsible member of your community to being involved in politics and voting. Most people think of their community as relating to their local neighborhood. As a member of a community, you have certain rights and responsibilities that range from voting to taking out your garbage and recycling according to the schedule set by your local government. Politics and voting cover every aspect from school board elections to electing the president of the United States.

SETTING REALISTIC GOALS

In ACT, there's a strong relationship between your values and the goals you set for yourself. Setting clear, attainable goals can help you tremendously in managing your stress. When your goals mirror your values, this helps you further reduce your stress because it helps minimize the discrepancy between what is most important to you (your values) and the direction of your life (your goals). In this section, you'll see how to set clear, attainable goals that mirror your values.

Having clear, attainable goals is an excellent way to organize your life around your values and reduce your stress. However, setting ambiguous or unattainable goals that don't clearly support your values can actually become a source of stress. The same is true of goals that aren't your own but are designed to please others.

Realistic goals are rooted in small steps that set you up for success. Goals such as finishing college, starting your own business, buying a house, having a baby, and so on, reflect your values and revolve around behavior, not just talk. To clarify your values and realize your goals, you need to take action. It's not enough merely to dream about what you want. You have to do the work. When you reach your goals, it validates what you value and motivates you to take on more difficult goals.

Unrealistic goals, however, work just the opposite way and set you up for failure. If you continually fail to reach your goals because they are unrealistic or unattainable, it can reinforce doubts or negative beliefs that you have about yourself and your abilities.

The best way to ensure that your goals are met is to set concrete, measurable objectives for each goal. Establishing measurable objectives helps you stay focused when you start to get lost in the process of doing the actual work. Think of a long-term goal you have for yourself. When you get bogged down in the process of working toward the goal, do you often stop and ask yourself, *So why am I doing this?* Measurable objectives give your goal more structure and allow you to stay focused and assess whether you're making any progress.

Measurable objectives basically answer this question: "Who will do how much of what by when?" Imagine that one of the things you value in the financial category is being your own boss and owning your own retail business in five years. A great way to track your progress is to set yearly objectives for things such as writing your business plan, gaining retail experience, and saving money as collateral for a small business loan. Here is a measurable objective for such a goal: "By the end of 2012 [by when], I [who] will save $5,000 [how much] to serve as collateral for a $50,000 small business loan [what]."

It takes practice in order to be comfortable writing measurable objectives. Don't cut corners and leave out parts of the formula. It's much harder to track your success if your objectives aren't measurable.

AN ACT-BASED FRAMEWORK FOR VALUES CLARIFICATION

Now that you have a clearer understanding of setting realistic goals, let's get back to values clarification. I've developed a values clarification model that integrates the four components of values clarification with basic ACT concepts about how your mind works. The resulting seven-step model is generic so you can use it to clarify your values related to all of the ten categories we discussed above. The following activity, ACTing to Clarify My Values, will help you practice identifying and clarifying your values.

VALUES CLARIFICATION ACTIVITY:
ACTing to Clarify My Values

Pick one of the values categories discussed in the Categorizing Your Values section above. You might consider choosing one that you feel contributes the most to your stress or that contributes the most to keeping you stuck in a rut. Identify one value for the category you chose and work through this one before moving on to a second value. This will help you keep your values straight.

Fill in the information required for each of the steps in the worksheet below, being as honest with your answers as possible. If you have any questions about how to fill out the worksheet, you may find it helpful to read through the sample that follows the worksheet.

When you're finished clarifying one value, you can move on to a second value in the category or switch to a different values category. Don't worry if you can't identify your values for a specific category. Accept this and move on to the next one until you've clarified your values for the remaining categories.

STEP 1: EXPLORE WHAT YOU VALUE

Some of the things that I value about [pick a category] are:

_____

_____

_____

STEP 2. CHOOSE AND RANK A VALUE

A value from this category that I'd like to explore further is:

_____

_____

_____

On a scale of 1–10 (1 = least important; 10 = most important) for all of my values, this value is a:

_____

STEP 3. PUBLICLY AFFIRM

Some of the things I can do to affirm this value to others are:

_____

_____

_____

STEP 4. TAKE ACTION

Some of the things I can do to demonstrate this value to others are:

_____

_____

_____

STEP 5. IDENTIFY THE THINGS THAT MAKE IT DIFFICULT TO AFFIRM AND ACT ON YOUR VALUES

The thoughts, personal scripts, scary pictures, or emotions that make it difficult for me to speak about this value or act on it are:

_____

_____

_____

_____

STEP 6. IDENTIFY WHAT YOU'RE WILLING TO ACCEPT

I'm willing to accept the following things in order to affirm and act on this value:

_____

_____

_____

_____

STEP 7. SET GOALS AND OBJECTIVES FOR AFFIRMING AND ACTING ON THIS VALUE

For this value, I'm willing to set the following goals and objectives:

Affirmation Goal

_____

_____

_____

_____

Objectives

a. _____

_____

_____

b. _____

_____

_____

c. _____

_____

_____

Action Goal

_____

_____

_____

_____

Objectives

a. _____

_____

b. _____

_____

c. _____

_____

Depending upon your time frame for meeting your goal, periodically (for example, daily, weekly, or monthly) review the progress you're making in meeting your objectives for reaching your goal. You might decide to change the time frame or add or delete an objective. While goals and objectives help give your life structure and help you clarify your values, they should also be flexible enough to adapt to changes in your personality and your life.

I suggest that you start with a simple goal, something that you can accomplish this week. By keeping the goal simple and the time frame manageable, you have a good chance of accomplishing it. I'll work through a family goal as an example:

STEP 1: EXPLORE WHAT YOU VALUE

Some of the things that I value about my family are:

- sharing information about what's going on in my life
- keeping up with events in family member's lives
- enjoying holidays together
- helping my sister out when she has a problem
- spending time with my nephews and nieces

STEP 2. CHOOSE AND RANK A VALUE

A value from this category that I'd like to explore further is:

On a scale of 1–10 (1 = least important; 10 = most important) for all of my values, this value is a: **10**

STEP 3. PUBLICLY AFFIRM

Some of the things I can do to affirm this value to others are:

- tell my family members how much I value them
- tell my friends how much I value my family
- when this subject comes up with colleagues at work, let them know how I feel

STEP 4. TAKE ACTION

Some of the things I can do to demonstrate this value to others are:

- write a letter to my sister and to my mother and father

- call my sister and my mother and father to ask what's going on in their lives

- invite my sister and her children over more often

- invite my sister, father, and mother over for Thanksgiving or Christmas

- call my sister and offer to help her when she has a problem

- invite my nephews and nieces to stay with me or take them on a weekend get-away

STEP 5. IDENTIFY THE THINGS THAT MAKE IT DIFFICULT TO AFFIRM AND ACT ON MY VALUES

Thoughts: *I'm still the young, single, irresponsible kid in the family. No one takes me seriously. They should be calling me up. They should be inviting me over since they have more room in their houses than I do in my apartment.*

Personal Scripts: *I still have this image of me being the kid sister with no responsibilities, always scuffling and totally spontaneous. I don't see myself as stable, future oriented, or a real family person since I'm not married with kids of my own. I still see myself as my parent's child rather than an adult on equal terms with them.*

Scary Pictures: *I always see my parents being very critical of me. I see this one picture of me with my head down, standing in the kitchen of my parents' house after they have just berated me about my poor report card. They did this in front of my sister, who always got straight A's. I always get this picture when I think of taking a trip back home to visit my parents and my sister and her kids.*

Emotions: *I get very anxious when I think of contacting my parents or my sister. I worry that they won't accept my attempts to reach out to them—or worse, they'll criticize me for not staying in touch.*

STEP 6. IDENTIFY WHAT YOU'RE WILLING TO ACCEPT

I'm willing to accept the following things in order to affirm and act on this value:

- Feeling anxious and worried

- Being rejected

- Having my stressful thoughts, scripts, and scary pictures roll around in my head while I take action

STEP 7. SET GOALS AND OBJECTIVES FOR AFFIRMING AND ACTING ON THIS VALUE

For this value, I'm willing to set the following goals and objectives:

Affirmation Goal

To let my sister and my parents know that being in contact with them is important to me.

Objectives

a. *By the end of next week, I'll call my sister and tell her that I value her being a bigger part of my life (this is all I can handle right now).*

Action Goal

To invite my nieces to spend a long weekend with me in the city.

Objectives

a. *By the end of next month, I'll talk to my sister about inviting my nieces to visit me.*

b. *By the end of next month, I'll go over my nieces' school schedule with my sister to identify a weekend where they have a Friday or Monday off.*

c. *By the end of next month, I'll invite my nieces to spend a long weekend with me in my apartment in the city.*

As you can see in this example, one value can manifest itself in many ways. By narrowing your focus and limiting yourself to one specific thing, you have a much better chance of accomplishing your goal. Once you accomplish this family goal, you can move on to other family goals. Sometimes accomplishing one goal not only gives you the confidence to take on another, it also opens the door to other possibilities that you didn't even foresee when you set out on your original plan. For example, you might learn after taking your nieces to a museum that they're fascinated with Italian art. You talk to your sister about this and find out that she also loves it. This exchange leads the two of you to start talking about the possibility of taking a vacation to Italy together. You love traveling and are also smitten with Italian art. This kind of synergy isn't uncommon as you plan and meet your goals.

Before you continue reading, it would be very helpful if you went back and used the information and exercises in this section to clarify your values related to all ten values categories. This will give you a lot of insight that you can apply to the information and exercises in the remainder of the book. Since the foundation of ACT is based on taking valued action, this will be time well spent.

AN ACT PERSPECTIVE ON VALUES

Now that you have clarified your values, you can see how they represent what's most important to you and how they define who you are as a person. You also have a better sense of why values conflicts can be so stressful. When someone or some situation threatens something you value, it's as if all of you is being threatened, not just that part of you that's connected to the value. While your values offer a look into your soul and who you are as a person, any one value is just a small part of you, the whole person. While this may seem contradictory, what I mean is that you are greater than just a single value and even greater than the sum total of all that you value.

As you learned in chapter 2, ACT revolves around how your mind functions in different contexts. While most people view values as fixed and immutable, those of us who subscribe to an ACT perspective tend to view them as more fluid. Remember, ACT helps you look at how useful your thoughts, emotions, and behavior are in the service of your values and the goals you have set for yourself. You can take this one step further and examine the relevance and usefulness of your values at any point in your life.

You're probably thinking, *Now wait a second, just a minute ago you said that my values are central to defining who I am as a person and set the stage for all of my goals. Now you're saying that they're fluid and constantly changing to suit the situation.* My answer to that is yes and no. I'm saying that your values mirror your personality and guide the goals and objectives you set for yourself. I don't feel, however, that they constantly change—they just bend a little. I like to think of values like trees. They have deep roots that nurture them. They have many branches that reach out and have no limits regarding where they can spread and how far they can grow. In times of stress, they can bend without breaking. They can slough off adversity (just as trees slough off ice or snow), spring back, and continue to grow. In other words, like the flexible tree and its branches, your values can bend without breaking if you have sufficient psychological flexibility.

I like to think of your values as fluid—that they're able to adjust and serve you rather than being fixed and requiring you to adjust and serve them. Many internal conflicts arise when you realize that you've outgrown a value and need to either modify it, cut it loose, or adopt a different one to replace it. There's nothing morally wrong with doing this. You're constantly changing and evolving as a human being. It simply doesn't make sense to think that your values aren't capable of changing and evolving if you allow them to. Unfortunately a lot of people confuse this with going against their values because they view them as a fixed commodity capable of being interpreted only one way. Instead of viewing their changing values as going *with* their lives and experience, they see them as going *against* what they stand for. Values can be interpreted to mean different things under specific circumstances and in different contexts at varying points in your life.

Let's use human life as an example. What do you value regarding human life? This question has been raised in discussions ranging from war to abortion to euthanasia, just to mention three areas. Let's examine how your values regarding human life might be expressed when dealing with the subject of euthanasia. Imagine you're seventeen years old and you have a neighbor who's in the hospital with a terminal form of cancer. At this point in your life, you might say something like this: "I believe doctors should do everything within their power to keep sick people alive as long as they can. You never know if they might find a new way to cure cancer." Imagine that, at twenty-seven years old, you experience the loss of a friend at work who suffered from a different—and long—terminal illness. On his passing, you say, "It's a shame my friend had to suffer so much until his life ended." Now imagine that you're fifty-seven years old and you watch your eighty-seven-year-old mother die in a nursing home from multiple chronic illnesses and dementia. Following a debilitating heart attack and stroke at eighty, which left her unable to eat, bathe, or walk on her own, you've watched her physically waste away and sink into a deep depression. She's told you on several occasions over the past few years that she wishes she were dead. Recently you've found yourself saying, "I just can't see how it's humane to keep my mom alive against her own will when she's in such pain and is suffering so much. I think it would be so much more humane to just let her end her life and die with whatever dignity she has left."

All three of these statements represent different points of view regarding what you value about human life. At fifty-seven, your views are different from what they were when you were seventeen. You realize that your values have changed as your own life and experience have given you a greater understanding of the issue. While you still value human life, you realize that this can be expressed in a variety of different ways. You realize that at age seventeen, you had very little personal experience with suffering and death, and your values about life were really those of your parents. At twenty-seven, living on your own, you had your first personal exposure to the death of a friend. Watching this person suffer and eventually die changed the way you perceived life and death. At fifty-seven, with a wife and family of your own, you watched your mother become incapacitated and suffer. Once again you realized that while you still greatly value human life, you're no longer so certain that preserving it at all costs and under all circumstances is the best way to express this value.

From a purely secular point of view, none of the three positions devalues human life. Each functions according to the context of the terminal illness and your own life and experience. These positions on your values continuum of human life interact with other values you have about things such as religion, the law, your family, and your culture (to name just a few). Your position also reflects your relationship to the person with the terminal illness. As the relationship changed (from your neighbor to your friend to your mother), so did the context and the function of your value.

Approaching values from an ACT-based perspective of how they function in a particular context might be very difficult for you if you have strong religious values that look at things such as the value of human life in a very inflexible way. In many instances, religious values are one dimensional and aren't open to interpretation depending upon the context. Rather than being fluid and flexible, they're rigid and inflexible. I'm not saying that this is good or bad—it just is. You need to decide for yourself whether such a view of specific values is helpful or unhelpful for you in managing your stress. In the next chapter, I'll discuss the role of spirituality in values clarification and provide a couple of different tools to help you sort through this.

FUSING WITH YOUR VALUES

Sometimes when you get stuck because of a values-related issue, it's because you've fused with a value that no longer works for you or that's causing a conflict. Sometimes you've simply outgrown the value and it's no longer helpful in meeting your goals. Other times the value you've fused with is still important and has meaning for you, but it puts you in conflict with others. In any case, you want to move forward, but your old value keeps you stuck and you can't find a way out of your problem. When this happens, you *become* the value rather than just viewing it as one part of your being. As a result, you have a hard time stepping back and looking at the conflict clearly.

Values conflicts crop up constantly. They're often triggered by the expectations or actions of others. For example, imagine that honesty is something you value and you just took a new job. You don't believe in cheating others regarding money, even if you can get away with it. At work, you're allowed to write off a certain amount of money each month because you use your personal automobile for work-related travel. After the end of the first month, you hand in your expense account and your boss calls you into a meeting regarding your travel expenses. You can't imagine what could possibly be wrong, because you kept scrupulous records of your mileage, parking, and tolls. When he meets with you, he explains that most of the workers have expenses that are twice yours for the same amount of work and you're making them look bad by handing in such a low expense voucher. Without directly asking you to do so, your boss wants you to pad your expense account so the other workers won't get into trouble. This puts you right in the middle of a values conflict between what you value regarding honesty and money and what your boss is asking you to do. You can see how this type of values conflict can be very stressful.

You might find the following activity, The Values Whiteboard, extremely helpful in allowing you to step back and view what your mind is telling you about a value that you've fused with. This activity is an adaptation of The Whiteboard activity introduced in chapter 2.

DEFUSION ACTIVITY: The Values Whiteboard

Instructions

1. Identify the underlying value in your current values conflict as clearly as possible.

2. Say to yourself, *My mind is telling me the following things about this values conflict,* and then—using a whiteboard, flip chart, or sheet of paper—write down everything your mind tells you about this conflict. Make sure to include both individual words and personal scripts regarding the values conflict.

3. Say to yourself, *I see the following scary pictures regarding this values conflict,* and then close your eyes and attend to the exact mental images that you see in your mind's eye. Write them all down exactly as you see them.

4. Say to yourself, *I feel the following emotions and body sensations regarding this values conflict,* and then write down these emotions and body sensations.

5. Now step away from the board, chart, or paper. Put at least six feet of distance between the board and your body. Say to yourself, *My mind really has a lot to say about this values conflict—how interesting.*

6. Do not judge or evaluate what your mind tells you. Instead ask yourself the following question: *How helpful is any of this in managing my stress and meeting my goals?* Write your answer on a different part of the board, chart, or paper.

7. Ask yourself, *What am I willing to accept about this conflict in order to move forward to live my life and meet my goals?* Write your answer on a different part of the board, chart, or paper.

In time and with practice, you'll find that distancing yourself from what your mind tells you about the value and the conflict you're experiencing will help defuse it. When this happens, you can begin to view the value and the conflict as parts of you that exist in their own contexts and with their own functions. In the next chapter, you'll learn how to use your values to live a life that is more consistent with your goals and what gives you meaning.

The key to managing values conflicts is being able to clearly identify your value(s), the nature of the situation that's causing the conflict, and how your options for clearing up the conflict relate to your goals. As you saw in the example about honesty, some conflicts also introduce additional elements like cheating, breaking the law, and other issues that can lead to consequences that stretch beyond resolving your stress. The decision you make regarding how to clear up the values conflict also needs to take these other issues into consideration.

❧

Staying true to your values, setting goals, writing measurable objectives, and analyzing values conflicts is a lot of work. You might even find it stressful at times as you try to work through this material. It's very important, however, and if you do the work now, it will reap big dividends down the road because you'll be laying the foundation for a stress management program that is based on what you care most about in life. It won't be somebody else's cookie-cutter approach to generic stress management. All of the things you'll learn in the rest of this book will help you stay true to your values and on course with doing the things that will help you meet your goals.

CHAPTER 5

Purposeful Living Through Valued Action

A hallmark of high-level mental well-being is feeling comfortable with who you truly are as a person and living a life that is consistent with this. This means knowing yourself and not having to justify to others who you are, what you think, or how you feel. It means accepting your weaknesses along with your strengths and being responsible for your actions.

Mental well-being also means striving to minimize role playing or acting in ways that aren't consistent with who you are and what you believe in. I've intentionally chosen the word "minimize" here because I firmly believe that it's impossible to completely eliminate role playing. For example, if you want to keep your job, you have to adhere to a set of rules and regulations regarding "appropriate" work-site behavior (everything from following a dress code to parking in designated spots). If these rules and regulations aren't consistent with your own values regarding clothing and parking, you're essentially playing the role required of you as an employee of this company. Complying with these rules and regulations might rub you the wrong way, but they don't compromise your core values, so you go along and follow the rules because you basically like the job and value it more than your taste in clothing and your desires about parking. If the rules and regulations do violate your most important values and you feel that this represents too much of a discrepancy between who you are and what you need to do to keep this job, you might consider resigning.

The goal of a purposeful life is to be as genuine as possible regarding your core values, understanding that at times you have to go along with things that you don't like but which don't go against what you hold most dear. Understanding how your values relate to the greater purpose of your life is the next level of values clarification and goal setting.

PURPOSEFUL LIVING AND GOAL SETTING

When I ask students and clients, "What is your purpose in life?" most of them look at me strangely and assume it's some kind of trick question. Others stop, look to the heavens, scratch their heads, and say, "Purpose—you mean like, what's my plan?" or "What's the meaning of my life?" Usually they follow this with "Gee, I've never really thought much about it."

Those who have thought about it often describe their purpose in terms of their goals. These people relate their purpose to their careers, family, or work goals. They'll answer with statements such as "I'm planning on going to law school and becoming a lawyer," "I'm engaged and getting married next year," or "I'm working on a demo CD and trying out for *American Idol* next year." Others have more altruistic purposes and say things like "I want to give something back to my community," "I want to work to save the environment," or "I want to stop the war in the Middle East." Still others have a more hedonistic purpose and say, "I just want to have fun" or "I just want to travel and see the world." As you can see, your purpose in life is very personal and can be defined in many different ways.

Most formal definitions of the word "purpose" revolve around the concept of intent. When you do something on purpose, you *intentionally* do it. You don't do it by chance, or on a whim, or because of fate—you do it because it's your intention to act this way. *Purposeful living* refers to your ability to intentionally live your life the way you set out to, according to your values, goals, and plans.

From a purely stress management perspective, purposeful living doesn't mean having the "right" purpose as defined by others. It means having a purpose that meshes with who you are and what you value. When you have no purpose in life, you're like a sailboat without a rudder, subject to the whim of the wind. The wind is often unpredictable, blowing this way and that, taking you along with it. Sometimes the wind is still and you sit, waiting for the tides to carry you wherever they will. Like the rudderless sailboat in the wind, when you have no purpose in life, the tide controls where you go—you can be lost at sea or get stuck on a sandbar. It's stressful to be "rudderless," so finding your purpose in life is central to ACTing to manage your stress.

A FINAL WORD ON PURPOSE

In *The Happiness Trap*, Russ Harris (2007) warns about getting stuck when your purpose is to avoid pain and discomfort. The happiness trap is built on the premise that it's possible, even desirable, to avoid pain and suffering. I hope by now you can see that this is a fallacy. As we discussed in chapter 2, avoidance is very tempting but also very limiting. Remember, one of the tenets of ACT is that life *is* troubling, confusing, and painful at times. A purposeful life doesn't run and hide when the going gets tough. It doesn't avoid difficult experiences—it embraces and accepts them willingly. In the short run, it's easier to run from your fears, pain, and suffering than to accept them for what they are, coexist with them, and get on with doing the things you need and want to do in your life. But in the long run, few people realize their dreams and live a valued life without accepting the fears, pain, and suffering that accompany them on their life journey. All of the meaningful accomplishments in life that you've earned have been accompanied by suffering. In fact, some of your accomplishments wouldn't mean as much to you if they came too easily.

If your purpose in life is just to have fun and avoid things that cause you pain or discomfort, this will work against ACTing to manage your stress. If you are willing to accept your suffering, there are two interesting approaches you can use to examine your purpose in life. One involves looking forward in your life to where you think it will take you. The other involves imagining that you're looking back on your life, revisiting what your life could have been. Both are designed to give you some structure for examining your purpose. Let's start by looking forward.

USING DAILY LIFE CRITERIA TO FIND YOUR PURPOSE

An interesting way to understand your purpose in life is to assess what it means to you to have a "good" day or a "stress-free" day. Generally your good days are those that are free from any major threats to your values and lifestyle. These are days of minimal role playing and few compromises regarding who you are and what you believe in. Stress-free days usually involve doing the things that have value and personal meaning for you and that bring you happiness. They usually include engaging in fun activities where time just seems suspended. While these days might have their ups and downs, the negative aspects are generally offset by the overall goodness of the day. I believe that these days are good for you because they represent a state where you have either no or minimal conflict between what you value in life and how you actually live your life. This is an idyllic state where who you truly are and what you do mesh seamlessly for a short period.

Linda Anderson Krech and Gregg Krech (2005) call this a day in which you meet your "daily life criteria" (DLC) for happiness and purpose. Your *daily life criteria* are your standards for living life well. For the most part, your DLC are concrete activities that you engage in on a regular basis. The way you would live your life on an ideal day is a reflection of what you value most in life. Some examples of DLC are making love with your partner, spending the day at the beach, reading a good book, making some money in the stock market, voting for the candidate of your choice, going to the theater, getting in a good workout, and so on.

Your daily life criteria set standards for what is truly important to you and what you intend to do with your life. The more you intentionally live in harmony with your DLC, the less stress you'll experience, because you're being true to yourself and what you value in life. Here's another simple activity, called A Stress-Free Day, that will help you examine what you really want and need to be happy and in control of your stress.

VALUES CLARIFICATION ACTIVITY:
A Stress-Free Day

Imagine what a perfectly stress-free day for you would be like. Where would you be living? Who would you be living with? What kind of work (paid or otherwise) would you be doing? Who would you be doing it with? What kinds of other activities would it include? Would you write, sing, run, create, make love, cook extravagant meals, or serve simple meals to others in a soup kitchen?

Be as specific as possible. In other words, instead of saying "I'd get some exercise," say "I'd ride my bicycle" or "I'd take my time and lift weights for a full ninety minutes."

I'd be living _____

I'd be living with _____

I'd be doing the following work _____

I'd be working with _____

I'd also do the following things:

_____

_____

_____

_____

_____

Now consider these questions:

1. *How do these daily life criteria reflect my values?*

_____

_____

_____

_____

2. *How does my typical day compare to this stress-free day?*

_____

_____

_____

_____

3. *What stands in the way of my meeting these daily life criteria?*

_____

_____

_____

_____

Your daily life criteria capture how you would prefer to spend your time based on what you value most in life. They take your values out of the realm of ideas and put them into action. This is the key to living a purposeful life.

You usually start out with the best intentions for living your life according to what you value. As a child, you went to the movies, watched television, listened to music, and poured over websites, magazines, and other material thinking about the kind of person you wanted to be and the kind of life you wanted to lead. You dreamed of, hoped for, and set the stage for the kind of life you wanted to live—and then somehow you got stuck in the kind of life you're currently living. You ask yourself, *When did it start? How did that happen? Where did I go wrong?* Why not turn it around today? Why not live your life the way you intended it to be, with the meaning and passion you deserve? You can take that first step today. There's nothing holding you back except your stressful thoughts, outdated personal scripts, scary pictures, and painful emotions. The following defusion activity, Sail Away, is designed to help you separate from the things that keep you stuck in a life that is inconsistent with your purpose.

DEFUSION ACTIVITY: Sail Away

Imagine you're getting ready to sail away on a cruise. This cruise is different from any other one that you've ever taken. This is literally the trip of your life. This is the trip from where you are now to where you want to be in your life. Imagine that your destination is that place that exists in your stress-free day, which you described above.

What stressful thoughts, outdated personal scripts, scary pictures, and painful emotions will accompany you on this trip? List them here:

Stressful thoughts _____

_____

_____

Outdated scripts _____

_____

_____

Scary pictures _____

_____

_____

Painful emotions _____

_____

_____

Take each of these thoughts, scripts, scary pictures, and emotions and pack them away in a big steamer trunk. You won't need them, but they're still coming along on this journey. Put them all together, but take time to carefully examine them. Wrap each of them in newspaper and gently place them in the trunk.

When you get to your ship, tell the luggage handlers to stow this steamer trunk in the deepest hold because you won't need this baggage while you're on this journey, but it has to come along anyway.

Once this baggage is stowed away, go up on deck. Get as high on the ship as you are comfortable with, as far away from your steamer trunk as possible. Lean on the railing, close your eyes, and breathe in the crisp, salty air. Feel the sun on your face and the wind in your hair as your ship sets sail on the cruise of your lifetime. Think of all the wonderful things you want to do on this journey. There's nothing holding you back; you're free from the thoughts, outdated scripts, scary pictures, and painful emotions that have stood in your way all of these years. Don't worry—if you need your excess baggage, it's in the ship's hold, safely tucked away.

You begin your journey and feel both thankful for and liberated from all of the things that have brought you to this point. Each day of your cruise you meet new people and explore new ideas and places. You've never felt so free in all of your life, and you realize it's because for once you're living the way you always intended to.

At the end of your journey, you gather your things and take them to your new life. You've added much to what you brought along on the start of your journey. You almost forget about your steamer trunk. You realize that you can't leave it on the ship, so you take it with you when you depart.

When you arrive at your new home, you unpack some of your things and put them away in their new places. When you get to your steamer trunk, you decide to leave it locked and move it up to your attic, where it will stay and collect dust. You decide that it will always be there if you ever need the things inside, but right now you've got too much to do and think about as you live your purposeful life.

Hopefully this activity showed you that you can start the journey of your purposeful life while still carrying the excess baggage of your past. It will always be there because it is part of who you are, but it doesn't have to have a prominent place. You can tuck it away in the hold of your mind, accept it, and be willing to continue on your journey.

In the next section, you'll take a look back on your life and consider how you want others to remember you. It's an excellent way to look at your values from a slightly different perspective.

LOOKING BACK ON YOUR LIFE

An interesting way to clarify your purpose in life is to look at it in terms of where you are and how much time you have left on the planet. How long is the rest of your life and how do you want to spend the rest of your days left on this earth?

In his book *How to Use Your Eyes*, James Elkins (2000), a professor and artist, talks about how quickly time passes and how easy it is to forget to really *see* the things that give your life meaning. He writes of his own experience of viewing a beautiful field of green grass. Until he wrote about that specific field of grass, he'd never really paid much attention to it. He explains how he figured that he had his whole lifetime to capture it on film if he ever really wanted to do so. When he actually sat down to write about how to really see grass, Elkins was shocked by how little time he actually had left in his life to observe this grassy field in all of its glory over the changing course of the seasons.

He calculated that he had a total of about thirty thousand days (the average American lifespan of slightly over eighty-two years) to appreciate grass or anything else on the planet. Grass would actually be in bloom on about ten thousand of those days. Since he was forty years old, he realized that he had used up more than half of his potential opportunities to view the grass. He realized that he had about thirty summers left to watch the grass. He further estimated that where he lived each summer had about sixty days of good weather. During that time, because of other normal daily commitments, he was able to spend only about twenty days actually getting outside and observing the grass. When he finished his calculations, he estimated that gave him about six hundred more chances in his lifetime to see the grass. Factoring in illness, normal aging, and other things that could cut into his opportunities, the number dropped even lower than that. This might seem like a lot of time and many opportunities until you realize how quickly these remaining days can slip away.

When you realize that your life on the earth is finite and how quickly time passes, it makes you stop and question how you want to spend your remaining time. How much do you want to spend doing things you really don't want to do? How much do you want to spend in relationships that are not fulfilling, with people who drag you down? Wouldn't you prefer to fill each precious day with activities you value and that give your life meaning and fulfill your purpose? It's up to you.

Linda Anderson Krech and Gregg Krech (2003) used Elkin's example to develop a wonderful activity called Thirty Thousand Days to help you put this in perspective. The following activity—How Do You Want to Spend the Rest of Your Thirty Thousand Days?—is adapted from theirs. The activity is designed to help put your life and time into clearer focus and help you decide on the things you might want to abolish.

VALUES CLARIFICATION ACTIVITY:
How Do You Want to Spend the Rest of Your Thirty Thousand Days?

Instructions

1. Calculate the exact number of days you've lived so far. Count the number of full years you've lived up until this year and multiply those by 365. Next add up all the days (including today) that you've lived this year.

2. Subtract this number from 30,000. This is the approximate number of days you have left on earth.

3. Make up the following three lists: (a) things I want to start doing, (b) things I want to continue doing, and (c) things I want to stop doing.

4. Describe how you want to spend the rest of your life, using information gathered from these three lists.

5. What are the stressful thoughts, outdated personal scripts, scary pictures, and painful emotions that are keeping you from doing this?

6. What are you willing to accept, and take action in spite of, among the things you listed in step 5?

I've found that this activity has more meaning the older you are. The first time I did it, I was blown away by how powerful it was. I'd lived more than half of my life and realized I was still doing things I didn't want to do. I also realized that I was spending time with people who brought me down and didn't contribute to my life's purpose. I've found that students and clients in their forties and fifties react the same way.

Sometimes younger people aren't as moved by this activity's power. My nineteen-year-old students and clients have a hard time relating to the urgency of its message because so much of their lives lie ahead of them. If the activity doesn't resonate for you at this point in your life, come back to it in a few years and try it again. In the meantime, share it with someone you love who's a little older and see if they benefit from it.

Another excellent but difficult way to look at the purpose of your life is to imagine that it's nearing its end and you're looking back and reflecting on it. What would you have built, written, recorded, created, and so on? What would you have accomplished? Who would you have loved? Where would you have lived? What would you leave behind for others to enjoy? What would your legacy be? How would others remember you?

One helpful way to do this is to write your eulogy, your life story that someone reads at your funeral. Your eulogy basically sums up your life one last time for all of those who've come to honor your passing into the next phase of your being. A few years ago I watched with admiration as my wife and her sisters worked on their mother's eulogy. My mother-in-law, Marie Riedel, was probably smiling as she watched her three daughters work with her minister, recounting the life of a simple woman—a mother, a wife, a devoted member of her congregation. Above all, however, Marie was a quilter. Read her eulogy and you'll see what I mean.

Eulogy for the Memorial Service of
Marie Riedel (1915–2003)

It has been said that you know someone more by what they choose to do than by what they have to do. We all have to work. Sometimes we choose our work with intentionality and what we do becomes a reflection of our interests and perhaps even our personality. But often we fall into work situations, making a choice because we have to earn a living, only to discover later that we may not like it but we have to do it. In this sense, what we choose to do gives us more insight than what we have to do.

Marie was a quilter. It was her pastime and her recreation. It is a deliberate and exacting craft to quilt. A pattern is envisioned. Fabric is chosen and cut into squares, and each is stitched to another. Batting is added. The fabric is put into place and the quilting begins. The running stitch draws the backing fabric together with the batting and intricate squares of color. It is this stitch, the running stitch, that is exact and deliberately made. It outlines the colorful square, fixing the pattern to the batting. Tiny stitches are carefully sewn. It requires patience. It isn't a craft for those of us who rush but for those of us who find contentment in small things, as those small things give way to larger things—say squares of fabric to a quilt or minutes to a lifetime.

Marie was a quilter. She had the marked capacity for contentment. She wasn't agitated and she didn't aggravate. She seemed at peace with what life brought her. She found peace in her own living. She spoke softly. I, for one, can't imagine her shouting (though perhaps she did when her girls were young). But I can't imagine it. She seemed content, had patience enough to listen, wasn't as concerned (as some of us others are) about getting our own opinions out there.

Marie was a quilter. And, as each stitch contributed to the whole quilt, so she understood that each action and every deed done contributes to a whole life. And when enough stitches are made, we see a pattern—of generosity, of doing for others. It was driving the kids to swimming at 6:00 a.m. It was involvement with the Brownies and Girl Scouts. And meals cooked. And church on Sundays. It was evenings with Bill after the girls went to bed. It was Christmases and the first days of school and lunches packed and laundry done. It was Women's Association meetings.

And when enough stitches are made, we see a pattern—of generosity, of doing for others. But the pattern is unique. Underlying the pattern is a batting of independence. She'd do things for herself and on her own. She didn't want to be a burden, she'd tell us. And when she defined her daughters as wonderful, she'd quietly remark with regret (or perhaps disappointment) that they'd had to take care of her in some way because of her illness. She'd apologize to the nurses at the hospital for having to attend to her. Yet this was her own doing. As a quilt draws admiration and wonderment at the work done, Marie seemed to draw gratitude and grace from us.

The wonderful thing about people who quilt is that they spend so much time and energy on something to give away. What real quilter hoards each quilt for themselves? But rather, crib quilts are given to newborns and large quilts are given as wedding presents and quilts are pulled out of cedar chests and laid upon the bed awaiting a visitor who'd stay the night. They warm us and delight our eyes—these carefully constructed pieces of fabric and love. And who should know this fabric of love quilted by Marie but those who were her heart's delight—her family.

So there are memories of Marie watching her grandsons play sports or visiting with her family in Pittsburgh or loving enough to include her sons-in-law. There were phone calls, always short and to the point, but inquiring, "How are things going?" "How are things doing?"

But there are fine stitches in a quilt. There is a moment when the last stitch is made and the quilt is done. The diagnosis of pancreatic cancer was jarring to us as well as its prognosis of months remaining, not years. I do not know what Marie did with that knowledge of that prognosis. She didn't talk about it. Perhaps she thought that if she did, she'd appear needy, something she didn't want to be. But I think for Marie, eighty-eight years old, looking back on a life she'd found contentment in, a life of faith and grace, a life of quiet presence, of daughters well married and on their own.

For Marie, this is how the remaining stitches are to be made. Not with a sense of resignation or depression, but of a pattern coming to completion, as all things must, a moment when the work is done and it is all finished.

And yet there is a greater quilter than Marie or any of us. There is the one who takes all our lives and stitches them together into his quilt of purpose. What we are and what we have done is not lost, but God receives Marie and ultimately us to himself and we find ourselves in his presence. Quilted together by love into an amazing pattern of color and fabric, of works, and faith, Marie finds her place in this heavenly quilt this day. Amen.

—The Reverend John L. Tipton
   August 16, 2003
   Connecticut Farms Church
   Union, New Jersey

Most people don't like thinking about their own death, yet by pondering your mortality, you can gain a new understanding of your life and its purpose. Usually, writing your eulogy is done by someone close to you. Writing your own can be one of the most profoundly spiritual things you'll ever do. Take a moment and complete the following activity, The Life of...

VALUES CLARIFICATION ACTIVITY:
The Life of...

Imagine you are in the final days of your life. You still have all of your mental abilities, so you can look back and think clearly about the events of your life and the choices you made. Take a piece of paper and, in 250 words, write your eulogy. Write it in the third person, as if someone else is describing you and the life you led.

Now answer these questions:

 ∾ Who would you pick to read your eulogy?

 ∾ Where would you hold your funeral?

 ∾ What would your burial plans be?

 ∾ How do your eulogy and the answers to the questions above relate to your values?

SPIRITUAL CONSIDERATIONS OF PURPOSEFUL LIVING

While ACT is an empirically based form of psychotherapy and not a religious practice, there's a definite spiritual component to it because of the faith involved in accepting what you can't control. I think this spiritual connection is worth discussing, because you've probably struggled with clarifying your values and describing your purpose in life without thinking about how these things relate to your spirituality.

As you remember from the last chapter, spirituality is defined as a connectedness with something beyond the self. If you're religious, your sense of connectedness with something beyond your self probably starts with members of your faith community and God. If you have a secular sense of spirituality, this interconnectedness could manifest itself in many ways—with other people, all living things, nature, or the universe.

Regardless of how you define your spirituality, a key component of it is your faith. Faith is generally defined as the belief in something that cannot be proven empirically. For instance, you probably have faith in yourself and in your ability to succeed. You probably have faith in at least one member of your family and in your girlfriend, boyfriend, wife, husband, or partner. You have faith that they'll love and respect you and treat you kindly and with compassion. None of these things can be proven empirically because they all look forward into the future. For the most part, you base your faith in these people and your expectations of them on events from the past. If someone has treated you with love and respect, you have faith that they'll continue to do so into the future.

Faith is the cornerstone of spirituality. It's also the cornerstone of acceptance and willingness to take valued action and live a purposeful life. You have to have faith in order to accept and coexist with pain and suffering, be willing to make plans, set goals, and take valued action without knowing with certainty that things will ultimately work out and you'll get better.

In ACT, taking valued action can serve any goal. Your purpose in life could just as easily be accumulating wealth and material goods as it could meeting your spiritual needs. In essence, from an ACT perspective, your spiritual action would not be viewed any differently than taking any other type of valued action. If you're a deeply spiritual person, taking valued action probably transcends your self to serve others or a greater good. This represents a shift away from "doing what I want" to "doing what others need" or "doing what needs to be done for the greater good." When you coexist with painful thoughts and emotions by shifting your attention away from your self and onto purposeful activity, the focus of this behavioral shift could be in the service of others.

THE SERENITY PRAYER

On several occasions over the past couple of decades, Steve Hayes, the founder of ACT, has used the Serenity Prayer to illustrate the connection between acceptance and commitment on the one hand and spirituality on the other (Hayes 1984, 1994, 2004a, 2007). I remember the Serenity Prayer, carved into a wood plaque, sitting above my third-grade classroom chalkboard in public school in Newark, New Jersey: "God grant me the serenity to accept the things I cannot change, the courage to change those that I can, and the wisdom to know the difference."

In a sense, this little prayer captures the essence of acceptance and commitment. ACT clearly supports the first two components of the prayer. Acceptance of things you cannot change—like your past, and your thoughts, personal scripts, scary pictures, and painful emotions—is central to ACT. Being willing to take valued action—while coexisting with your stressful thoughts, scripts, scary pictures, and painful emotions—takes courage. ACT acknowledges this and helps you accept the pain and suffering inherent in your life while helping you find the courage to take valued action.

Where ACT differs from religious interpretations of the prayer is where the "wisdom to know the difference" comes in. The religious interpretation believes that God or some supernatural power provides the wisdom. In essence, a religious interpretation implies that if you follow the teachings of your religion, it'll provide the wisdom you need to know the difference. Using an ACT interpretation, the wisdom to know the difference doesn't come from the supernatural; it comes from contextual and behavioral science, which have provided the wisdom to know that the difference involves your behavior and your environment (Hayes 2001, 2004b). You learned all about this in chapter 3 when we discussed control. If you're serious about ACTing to manage your stress, it's important to keep coming back to this. You have the wisdom to know the difference between what you can and cannot change in your life. You can change your behavior and your environment despite the events of the past and the intellectual and emotional baggage that you carry around inside your head every day. You don't have to be a slave to your past or to any dogma that keeps you stuck and limits your psychological flexibility.

VALUES, SPIRITUALITY, AND THE SELF-AS-CONTEXT

In chapter 2, we talked about the differences between the self-as-context and the self-as-content. If you remember, according to ACT, any time you perceive a thought, feel an emotion, or experience a bodily sensation, you do so through the eyes of your observer self, the one that comprises the self-as-context. This is the *you* that has been around since you became fully conscious and is the end result of your genetic inheritance and social learning (nature/nurture) since the beginning of your life. This is the lens or filter through which you observe your internal world (your mind) and external world (your body and environment). You observe all thoughts, personal scripts, scary pictures, and painful emotions through this lens and become the context through which you view your world.

When you adhere to a self-as-context viewpoint, you see yourself as the perspective from which you *view* your thoughts, personal scripts, scary pictures, and painful emotions, rather than believing you *are* those things. This is the fundamental struggle that goes on in your mind that ACT is designed to help you with. Nowhere does the struggle between the self-as-context and the self-as-content occur more intensely than at the spiritual level. This is especially true if you're deeply religious, because this distinction is easily blurred. You might feel guilt, shame, or even sin for merely thinking about something that goes against your religious and moral values. Because of this, you might find it harder to adhere to a self-as-context perspective than someone who isn't religious.

The self-as-context from a spiritual perspective inextricably weaves the time spent in this life with time spent in the past and time that will occur in the future. If you're a Buddhist, for example, you regard this connection as being manifested through your karma. Your self is not only the sum total of your heredity and learning to this point in time, but it also contains your karma, because everything that you have experienced in your lifetime (even the fact that you are human) is influenced by your good or bad karma from the past. Taking valued action and living a purposeful life take on a different meaning when viewed through the context of relating to your karma. If you're a Christian, you consider your past to include original sin and your future to be infinite, extending beyond your years on earth to time spent in heaven, purgatory, or hell. Your self-as-context includes the sins of others and goes beyond your time spent on earth. This is very different from ACT, which is a secular therapeutic approach and not linked to any spiritual or religious traditions.

While this discussion of purposeful living uses Buddhism and Christianity as examples, you can substitute your own theology in their place. This also works if you have a more secular spirituality. For example, let's say that you don't believe in God and aren't a member of any formal religion, but you still feel that all humans are interconnected in some way. Your values and purpose might be strongly influenced by how your actions affect others and ultimately the earth and all living things who share the planet. Discussing purposeful living without acknowledging a spiritual connection is incomplete. The following activity, My Spiritual Connection, will help you sort through this.

VALUES CLARIFICATION ACTIVITY: My Spiritual Connection

Instructions

1. Think about one of your spiritual values and how it relates to your purpose.

2. Think about the stressful thoughts, outdated personal scripts, scary pictures, and painful emotions that you associate with this value and the actions you want to take to realize your purpose.

3. On a large piece of paper, make four columns. At the top of each column, write one of the following terms:

   ↩ Stressful thoughts

   ↩ Outdated scripts

   ↩ Scary pictures

   ↩ Painful emotions

   Under each heading, list what your mind is telling you.

4. Step at least three feet away from the paper and observe what your mind is telling you about these items.

5. Ask yourself, "How much psychological flexibility is there in my spirituality regarding these items?"

6. If you don't see much flexibility, ask yourself the following question: "How helpful are these thoughts, scripts, pictures, and emotions?"

7. If they're not helpful and they keep you stuck in self-defeating behaviors, keep coming back to them and use them in different defusion activities throughout the rest of this book.

If you have trouble defusing from your spiritual thoughts, scripts, pictures, and emotions, you might benefit from a meeting with your spiritual advisor to talk about these things.

❧

Earlier in this chapter you learned that the goal of a purposeful life is to be as genuine as possible regarding your values and your actions. Being as genuine as possible is one of the greatest steps you can take toward managing your stress. In the next chapter, you'll see how important this is when you're faced with stressful thoughts and painful emotions. Living a purposeful life can help you accept your pain and coexist with stressful thoughts while moving forward and meeting your goals.

CHAPTER 6

ACT, Acceptance, Willingness, and Experiential Avoidance

In the last two chapters, you learned about the importance of setting goals that reflect what you value in life. When you get stuck, you're either unsure of how to move forward or unwilling to take action to meet your goals. Sometimes all you need to do to get unstuck is to clarify your values and set clear goals and measurable objectives. In this case, getting stuck was simply due to not having a clear vision of what you wanted to do and how to accomplish it. Other times you need help in accepting what you're thinking or feeling in order to move forward. When your thoughts and emotions are stressful or painful, it's especially hard to be willing to move forward. Being willing to accept your pain and coexist with it while moving forward is difficult and takes practice. It's much easier to take a pill or avoid situations and people that are associated with your pain and suffering. ACT doesn't pull any punches regarding the nature of the work you have cut out for yourself. Developing acceptance and willingness is hard work and it is painful. If you stick with it, however, you'll find out that the struggle is worth it, and you'll become stronger and more psychologically flexible. This will help you manage your stress and future situations that cause you to temporarily get stuck again.

AN ACT VIEW OF ACCEPTANCE AND WILLINGNESS

In his book *Get Out of Your Mind and into Your Life*, Steve Hayes (2005) points out that acceptance and willingness deal with conditions that aren't easily changeable. In most cases, these conditions are the internal potential stressors that we discussed in chapter 3. Accepting the stressful thoughts, personal scripts, scary pictures, and painful emotions that at times flood your mind can seem overwhelming. Being willing to face these demons and move forward can seem like walking into a hurricane that threatens to topple you over and blow you away.

In many cases, you've carried around your stressful thoughts, unhelpful personal scripts, scary pictures, and painful emotions for years, and it's been very difficult to get rid of them. You've probably tried to avoid the situations that trigger them and to control or eliminate them when it was impossible to avoid them. The problem with doing this is that it keeps you stuck in unhelpful or destructive behavior patterns, and it limits your growth.

A Closer Look at Acceptance

Accepting something and being willing to move forward while coexisting with it doesn't mean you necessarily *want* it. It just means that you admit that it exists and you don't deny it. You accept the existence of the troubling thought, painful feeling, or whatever as a starting point for dealing with it. For instance, you might not like the anger you feel toward your boss, but you accept that it exists and are willing to work with him despite it. You accept the fact that you can be angry at something he said or did, and still respect him and be willing to work with him. This shows that you can be psychologically flexible and manage these seemingly contradictory positions.

You don't really want to feel angry at your boss (or anyone, for that matter), and you don't necessarily like the sensations that anger creates in your body. You realize that you'd prefer to feel something other than anger, but you accept it and are willing to move forward despite it.

Through acceptance, you acknowledge your humanity. Being human means being imperfect, making mistakes, contradicting yourself occasionally, losing your patience, and thinking or doing a thousand other things that you wish you hadn't done. Acceptance allows you to acknowledge your faults and imperfect moments and to keep moving forward while coexisting with them. Acceptance also involves being able to acknowledge your strengths and successes. Many people have a harder time accepting the positive and affirming aspects of their lives than the negative and troubling ones. Acceptance is about being real and acknowledging your life for what it is and your mind for what it's telling you. It takes courage to do this. The good news is that, even if you're not feeling very courageous now, you can develop courage at any point in your life. People of all ages do courageous things. You can start today to develop the courage you need to accept your life for what it is and move forward toward meeting your goals.

The following activity, I Am Willing to Accept..., is adapted from Hayes (2005).

ACCEPTANCE AND WILLINGNESS ACTIVITY:
I Am Willing to Accept...

Think about the internal potential stressors that now interfere with your ability to move forward and make progress toward your goals. Instead of trying to control these stressful thoughts, personal scripts, scary pictures, and painful emotions, list the ones you are willing to accept.

I am willing to accept the following stressful thoughts I have about myself and my life:

_____

_____

_____

_____

Trying to avoid the stressful thoughts listed above has caused for me the following negative consequences:

_____

_____

_____

_____

I am willing to accept the following negative personal scripts about my life:

_____

_____

_____

_____

Trying to avoid the negative personal scripts about my life listed above has caused for me the following negative consequences:

_____

_____

_____

_____

I am willing to accept the following scary pictures about my life:

_____

_____

_____

_____

Trying to avoid these scary pictures has caused for me the following negative consequences:

_____

_____

_____

_____

I am willing to accept the following painful emotions:

_____

_____

_____

_____

Trying to avoid these painful emotions has caused for me the following negative consequences:

_____

_____

_____

_____

A Closer Look at Willingness

In ACT theory and practice, acceptance and willingness are linked. You could view acceptance as being more related to your thoughts, while willingness is related to taking action. Think of acceptance as your mind telling you that when you encounter an internal potential stressor, it's okay to think, feel, and experience whatever you do think, feel, and experience. Willingness is your commitment to taking valued action while coexisting with the stressful thoughts and painful emotions you're experiencing.

An interesting metaphor for this is choosing to go out in a rainstorm. Rainstorms usually develop with some warning: you hear the weather report; see the clouds approaching; feel the changes in temperature, wind conditions, moisture, and so on; and feel the first light drops beginning to fall.

In most cases, when you know it's going to rain, you don't let the impending storm put an end to your daily activities, especially if they're things that are important to you and that connect to your values and goals (going to work, school, to see a loved one, and so on). Instead, you *manage* living with the rain. You can't change the rain, but you can change how you act in relation to the rain: you can control your own rain-related behavior. You can take several actions to coexist with the rain: you can wear rain gear (poncho, boots, or whatever), give yourself more time to get to where you're going, and use an umbrella to shield you from the raindrops.

Just as you manage living with the rain, you can also manage living with stressful thoughts, personal scripts, and painful emotions. The following activity, I'd Better Use My Umbrella, is a fun way to defuse from internal potential stressors.

WILLINGNESS ACTIVITY:
I'd Better Use My Umbrella

The next time you feel stressed because you can't cope with some internal stressor, identify the exact messages you're telling yourself about the situation. For example, *My mind is telling me I'll never learn how to manage my money and get out of debt, I can't stand feeling anxious over my bills,* and *I can't do anything right.*

Next, close your eyes and visualize the sky darkening, the wind picking up, and rain clouds swirling all around you. Now imagine that the messages your mind is telling you and any other stressful thoughts you have about the situation are like raindrops just beginning to fall on your head. You feel the drops and say to yourself, *I'd better use my umbrella.*

Imagine you have an umbrella. You open it and feel instant relief from the stressful thoughts, painful emotions, scary pictures, and bodily sensations. Like raindrops, they bounce off the umbrella and don't interfere with your doing what you need to do. As you continue "walking in the rain" with your umbrella, tell yourself, *Just as I can use an umbrella to help me manage living with real rain, I can use my acceptance and willingness "umbrella" to help me live my life while coexisting with unpleasant internal potential stressors.*

Any time you see the storm clouds of internal potential stressors on the horizon and anticipate becoming stressed by them, tell yourself, *I'd better use my umbrella,* and begin to view the stressful thoughts, painful emotions, scary pictures, and bodily sensations as raindrops bouncing off your umbrella as you go about your business.

Most of us would prefer to go about our business without having to walk in the rain. The reality of life, however, is that it will rain, snow, sleet, and send a lot of bad weather our way. You probably learned early in life that a little rain isn't going to make you melt, and even though you don't like it, it doesn't have to stop you from doing what you need to do. The bad weather also helps you appreciate those beautiful, warm, sunny summer days or the crisp, clear winter days when you feel so good just to be alive and to breathe in the clean air.

Willingness to Give Up Control

Kevin Polk (2008), a noted ACT therapist, trainer, and writer, describes how your desire to control your stressful thoughts, personal scripts, scary pictures, and painful emotions directly opposes your acceptance of them and your willingness to act. Polk describes two scales that come into play when you experience stress: a control scale and a willingness scale. He explains how these scales work in opposition to each other. When you turn the dial up on one, the other one automatically turns down. In other words, your control scale works in opposition to your willingness scale. When you "turn up the volume" on your control scale, your level of willingness automatically decreases. When you increase your willingness, the amount of control decreases. The more you try to control, avoid, or eliminate stressful thoughts, personal scripts, scary pictures, and painful emotions, the less willing you are to accept them and to take valued action. Hayes (2005) uses the analogy of dials on a radio as a metaphor for understanding this. In the following defusion activity, The Radio, I've built upon this notion of dialing up control and dialing down willingness (and vice versa) by connecting it to an old tabletop radio.

DEFUSION ACTIVITY: The Radio

Imagine an old-time tabletop radio. The radio is compact, has a single speaker, and has two dials on the front that control the tuning and the volume. Each dial has a scale from minimum to maximum (a scale of 1–10). When you want to increase the volume, you turn the dial from the lower number to the higher number. When tuning in a station, you turn the dial from the lower frequency stations to the higher ones.

Now, instead of those dials controlling volume and tuning, think of the two dials as representing control and willingness. The dial on the left is the control dial. The dial on the right is the willingness dial. As you turn up the control dial, you increase your desire to control, avoid, or eliminate your stressful thoughts, personal scripts, scary pictures, and painful emotions. As you turn up the willingness dial, you increase your acceptance of these things and your willingness to take valued action despite them.

The next time you have an internal potential stressor that you're trying to control or eliminate, imagine that you're turning up the control dial to its highest setting. Next, imagine how doing that makes you less willing to accept your discomfort and move forward taking valued action. The result? You get stuck.

Now imagine that you turn down the control dial and turn up the willingness dial, allowing yourself to accept your discomfort and coexist with it while you take valued action and make progress toward your goal. (Adapted from Hayes 2005.)

Whenever you get stuck and realize you're trying to control your stressful thoughts, personal scripts, painful emotions, or scary pictures, close your eyes and imagine the radio. Visualize putting your fingers on the control dial and turning it down, and then putting your fingers on the willingness dial and turning it up. You might want to say to yourself, *I'm having those old urges to control things. It is time to get out the old tabletop radio again.*

ACCEPTANCE, WILLINGNESS, AND CHANGE

As we've discussed already, one major reason you can't eliminate or control 100 percent of your stress is change: just when you think you have everything in your life under control, it changes. Your life and your potential stressors are constantly changing. This means that, despite your best efforts to control your life and your stressors, things change, throwing you out of balance and forcing you to adapt. If you're like most people, adaptation and change are threatening and difficult to cope with. Remember back to our working definition of stress: any time you find something threatening and beyond your ability to cope with, you'll be stressed.

Unfortunately change is a fundamental reality of all aspects of nature and life. The seasons change, ushering in times to plant and harvest. The weather changes, bringing with it much-needed rain, breaks from scorching heat, and refreshing wind. The landscape constantly changes as waves crash up on the beach, rivers rise and overflow their banks, and snow and ice erode seemingly impervious rocks and cliffs. Businesses change as they adapt to demands from the marketplace, innovations in science and technology, and new advances in production and distribution. People change as they adopt new technologies, integrate new information, and gain new knowledge and insights. If you stop and examine these and other examples of change, you'll see that in all aspects of life, change is the norm, not the exception.

Accepting change and viewing it as a healthy and growth-enhancing process in your life diminishes the threat associated with it and helps you to start believing that you *can* cope with it. If you feel that you can cope with change and not view all change as threatening, you will begin to develop greater psychological flexibility and view change as a challenge rather than a stressor. Once you can do this, change is no longer capable of sending you into a stress response.

Believing that change is the only constant in life isn't the same thing as believing in determinism. In other words, you can believe in the inevitability of change and not think that everything is predetermined and will change regardless of your plans. Believing that your life will frequently change doesn't mean that you have no control over it and that there's nothing you can do. Neither does it mean that you should stop trying to exert any control over your life. Rather it means you can start accepting that change is inevitable and that many changes are beyond your ability to control or eliminate.

Unfortunately most people view change as a threat and as something that they can't cope with because they can't control or eliminate it. It represents the great unknown and therefore is something to fear. Most people want to know what to expect so they can plan for the worst. If you worry that just when you achieve your goals, everything will change, you're likely to get stuck and not move toward your goals at all. Being willing to accept the inevitability of change and to take valued action while coexisting with this fact is a key step in ACTing to manage your stress. The following activity, Embracing Change, can help you examine the threat posed by any change you're facing and enhance your ability to cope with it.

ACCEPTANCE ACTIVITY: Embracing Change

During the next week, when you feel threatened by change or impending change in any aspect of your life, answer these questions:

- ☙ What is the exact change I'm facing?

- ☙ What is my mind telling me about this change?

- ☙ What outdated personal scripts do I have about change and my ability to handle it?

- ☙ What's the scariest picture my mind is showing me regarding this change?

- ☙ What sensations do I feel in my body as my emotions are aroused by this change?

- ☙ What specifically is threatening to me about this change?

- ☙ On a scale of 1–10, how threatening is this change?

- ☙ How have I coped with similar changes in the past?

- ☙ What can I do to prepare for this change?

- ☙ How much time do I have to prepare for this change?

- ☙ What can I do to adapt to this change once it occurs?

- ☙ How can I turn the threat associated with this change into a challenge?

- ☙ How can I grow by adapting to this change?

Use what you learn from answering these questions to help you defuse from your stressful thoughts and personal scripts regarding the role of change in your life. Use this information to set goals and objectives to take valued action despite the changes that will inevitably occur.

As you become more successful taking valued action while coexisting with your change-related fear and anxiety, you'll begin to defuse the mind-set that change is negative and threatening. Gradually you'll come to realize that change is not only inevitable, it's also a valuable and enriching part of your life. Change starts to become your friend, a renewing force that you can expect, anticipate, and even look forward to.

ACT AND EXPERIENTIAL AVOIDANCE

You've probably tried to reduce your stress by avoiding people, places, and situations that make you uncomfortable. In keeping with our threat-appraisal way of dealing with potential stressors, your discomfort is due to the threat, harm, or loss associated with those stressors and your belief that you can't cope with them. Regardless of which half of the appraisal model (threat or coping) is involved, your response to these potential stressors often involves trying to avoid them.

As you'll see in the example that follows, there are many different forms of avoidance behavior. Avoidance can focus on internal or external potential stressors. It can result in inaction (such as doing nothing in response to a stressor), or in unhelpful or harmful behavior (such as drinking or using drugs to avoid facing the stressor) or in helpful coping behavior (such as calmly asserting your needs). You may remember from chapter 3 that attempting to avoid, control, or eliminate *internal* potential stressors will result in making them worse. (To review, these internal potential stressors are the stressful thoughts, personal scripts, scary pictures, and painful emotions that your mind constantly churns out.) You do have some degree of control over your *external* potential stressors, your behavior, and your environment.

Let me give you an example of an unhealthy behavioral response used to avoid a threatening external potential stressor. Imagine that you have to go to court because of a serious traffic violation. You were caught speeding and given a summons that included a hefty fine, points attached to your driving record, and a mandatory court appearance. You're familiar with the municipal judge in your town and know that he always comes down heavy on people who are caught exceeding the legal speed limit by more than 25 mph. You're very threatened by this court appearance. You have already accumulated enough violation points on your record that you fear the judge will suspend your driver's license. If this happens, it'll be very difficult and expensive for you to get to work and take care of your family.

On the day you're required to appear in court, you decide that you can't handle the fear, shame, and guilt that you're feeling regarding having to appear in your town's municipal court for your speeding violation. On your way to court, at the last minute you decide that you're just going to avoid the whole thing. You turn around, drive to a local tavern, and spend the evening drinking. You come home at midnight and your wife is furious. She refuses to speak to you and makes you sleep in the den.

Obviously this is an overly dramatic example of the extremes that someone might go through to avoid the emotional distress and painful thoughts associated with a potential stressor. Someone else might have tried to avoid, control, or eliminate thinking about the court date. A different person might have had a few drinks or taken some psychoactive drugs prior to the court date to avoid the painful feelings of actually being in court and facing the judge.

What all of these people have in common is trying to avoid the potential stressor itself, or the thoughts or emotions associated with it. Jason Luoma and his colleagues (Luoma, Hayes, and Walser 2007) discuss three major types of behavior that people typically engage in when trying to avoid an experience: (1) internal avoidance behavior, (2) overt emotional control behavior, and (3) narrowing or constricting behavior. Let's take a quick look at each of these.

Internal avoidance behaviors try to avoid the potential stressor by attempting to control or eliminate the thoughts and feelings associated with it. Daydreaming, excessive worrying, and telling yourself to think or feel differently are examples of internal avoidance behaviors.

Overt emotional control behaviors try to avoid the potential stressor by attempting to distract you from it. Drinking, using psychoactive drugs, overeating, gambling, and engaging in thrill seeking are examples of overt emotional control behaviors.

Narrowing or constricting behavior is the intentional shutting off of direct experience. This could involve dropping out of activities that you perceive as stressors, even though there are aspects of them that you find enjoyable or rewarding. Another example would be limiting opportunities to engage in new activities and meet new people because this is perceived as threatening. When you intentionally narrow or constrict your opportunities to do new things and meet new people, you adhere to your rigid (but comfortable and known) patterns of behavior.

There is a fine line between healthy avoidance and unhealthy or unhelpful avoidance. It's unhealthy and unhelpful to avoid things that you need to do to reach your goals and live in harmony with your values. It's also unhealthy and unhelpful to be held prisoner to a rigid way of behaving when you realize that it isn't in your best interests and it's keeping you from realizing your full potential.

Avoidance, however, isn't necessarily bad. It can be a useful stress management skill when you avoid stressors that you know you could cope with if you wanted or needed to, but you choose to avoid them anyway. You avoid them because you know that they stand in the way of meeting your goals or they're in conflict with what you value. For example, let's say that you're against using marijuana. You've heard all of the pro-and-con arguments regarding occasional marijuana use, and you're convinced that it isn't any more harmful than occasional alcohol use. Unlike alcohol, however, it is illegal, and you refuse to get involved with illegal activity. Let's say you're very tired one evening. All you want to do is stay in and watch a ball game. Then a friend calls and wants you to get high with him and then go out barhopping. Avoiding this pot-smoking friend might be an excellent way to reduce your stress that evening.

In my previous books, *Coping with Stress in a Changing World* (2007) and *Seven Weeks to Conquering Your Stress* (2006), as well as in my work with clients and students, I've presented avoidance as a workable strategy when dealing with "type 1 stressors" that stand in the way of meeting your goals. *Type 1 stressors* are things that you can anticipate and avoid. They're external potential stressors, things related to your environment or your behavior and within your ability to control. When external potential stressors threaten you because they stand in the way of meeting your goals or they conflict with your values, it's perfectly acceptable to try to avoid them. Typically they're stressors that you know about in advance and have time to work with. (I'll discuss type 1, 2, and 3 stressors in greater detail in chapter 9.)

For example, imagine you go to the gym every Monday, Wednesday, and Friday evening from 6:00 p.m. to 8:00 p.m. Going to the gym is your way of staying in shape and winding down from your workday. Then you get invited to go to a party the following week with some colleagues from work. They want to carpool and leave directly from the office. You're feeling a little stressed out as you anticipate either missing your workout or telling your work colleagues (they're not really your friends) that you don't want to attend. You're not sure what you're going to do, but you have a whole week to decide. Ultimately you decide that you'll go to the party—but after you finish your workout. You'll also drive your own car so you can leave whenever you wish. In this case, you didn't avoid the entire experience, only aspects of it (missing your workout, having to carpool) that you found were threatening.

This example was pretty clear-cut. Most social and interpersonal potential stressors are not so clear-cut. When you avoid certain external stressors, you must be careful that you don't avoid potentially enriching or helpful situations just because they make you feel uncomfortable.

☙

ACT will help you become more mindful of when you engage in experiential avoidance. As you'll see in the next chapter, mindfulness training is designed to help you develop a greater awareness of your life on a moment-by-moment basis. The first step in understanding if your experiential avoidance helps or hinders your stress management activities is becoming more aware of when you're actually avoiding experiences. The second step, minimizing unhealthy experiential avoidance, comes with time and practice of the activities outlined in this chapter and the rest of the book. In time, you'll become better equipped to accept stressful thoughts, personal scripts, scary pictures, and painful emotions and rely less and less on using experiential avoidance to cope.

CHAPTER 7

Developing Mindfulness

In chapter 2, I introduced the concept of mindfulness and described how it's linked to acceptance and willingness, which set the stage for taking valued action. In order to accept potential stressors and move forward in life, you first must become aware of those stressors. One way to think of mindfulness is awareness training. When you're mindful of something—like your stressors—you're aware of it and give it your full attention. But why would you want to give your stressors your full attention? Let's take a closer look at what mindfulness is to learn why.

WHAT IS MINDFULNESS?

In *Mindfulness and Psychotherapy*, Christopher Germer (2005) defines *mindfulness* as "moment-by-moment awareness" (6). This simple but elegant definition eliminates most of the confusion related to other ways of defining mindfulness and really emphasizes the key point: being mindful of the present moment.

How do you know if you're being mindful of the present moment? According to Germer (2005), there are four key characteristics of mindful moments. They are (1) present centered, (2) nonjudgmental, (3) nonverbal, and (4) nonconceptual. Mindful moments always focus on the present, never the past or the future. Unlike most of your thoughts, which are often one step removed from the present—that is, you're thinking of either the past or the future—mindful moments always exist in the present space and time. Therapists like to call this being fully involved in the *here and now*. Mindful moments also always exist on a nonverbal level. I call this your *subvocal speech*, that is, the things you say to yourself. Verbalizing or writing down these subvocal messages adds an additional layer of interpretation and distance from them. And finally, mindful moments are not *thinking* moments where you try to figure something out or judge it. During mindful moments, you merely note the occurrence of something and accept it for what it is.

BECOMING MORE MINDFUL OF YOUR EXTERNAL ENVIRONMENT

Becoming more mindful starts with increasing your awareness of the present moment and paying more attention to it. A good place to start practicing mindfulness is by paying more attention to what's going on around you in the physical world, your external environment. Paying more attention, on purpose, to your external environment is a good way to become more aware of the things in it that are common sources of stress for you.

Being aware of the present moment and paying more attention to it are actually two different skills. You can be aware of something but not give it your full attention. This can happen for a variety of reasons. One reason is that you get distracted by something else. This is a common by-product of multitasking, where you are engaged in several things simultaneously, such as driving, drinking a cup of coffee, and talking on your cell phone. It's easier to get distracted when doing multiple things like this at the same time. Another reason for not giving your full attention to what you're doing is that your mind wanders back to the past or forward into the future. This commonly occurs when you're reading or writing, and your mind drifts to other thoughts about something that happened yesterday or that you've planned for tomorrow. In both examples, becoming distracted wasn't a conscious decision—your mind just shifted away from being fully involved in the present to being only partially mindful.

Paying attention to the present moment involves catching your mind when it shifts focus to the past or the future, and then redirecting your full attention back to what you're doing now. Think of paying attention to the present moment as being the opposite of being distracted. Paying attention to the present moment, on purpose, is a skill you can develop regardless of your age, intelligence, attention span, or any other factor.

Gregg Krech, the director of the ToDo Institute in Vermont, has been helping people hone this skill for years. He has written extensively on the subject and integrates it with the institute's mission of teaching people how to use Japanese psychotherapy and Buddhist principles to live more constructively. Four of Krech's (2005) basic assumptions about attention are (1) your experience is not based on your life, but on what you pay attention to; (2) what you pay attention to grows; (3) most of us exercise little voluntary control over our attention; and (4) working with your attention is a skill, and competence requires practice. Let's take a quick look at each of these assumptions.

Your experience of life is not based on your life, but on what you pay attention to. Think about this for a moment: although you might have been exposed to something, if you didn't pay attention to it, you missed it. Unlike the instant replay you've become accustomed to watching on television broadcasts of sporting events, you get only one shot at observing your life. This is why it's so crucial to start being more mindful of the present moment. Each moment is unique and full of detail, if you allow yourself to see it.

What you pay attention to grows. This has both positive and negative connotations and really connects with ACT theory. For example, paying attention to something beautiful and relaxing, like the sounds of birds in your garden, will heighten your awareness of them and help you discriminate between the various sounds they make. Paying too much attention to stressful emotions like anger and anxiety can actually fuel them and keep them alive longer than if you just accepted them and moved on.

Most of us exercise little voluntary control over our attention. American culture is enamored with television, video games, text-messaging, and other forms of communication that revolve around shortening, compressing, and speeding up the transmission of information. Growing up in this culture has trained you (and me) to expect things to move at an unnaturally fast pace. This unnaturally fast-paced environment makes it difficult to learn how to focus your attention on a single item for a sustained period. For example, a typical thirty-minute television show can easily compress a week's worth of time into one show. Texting uses abbreviated spelling patterns to make typing messages quicker and easier.

Working with your attention is a skill, and competence requires practice. Increasing your attention isn't mystical or impossible. It involves learning (or relearning) a skill. Anyone can do it if they work at it and practice regularly. One of the key benefits of mindfulness training is that it will increase your ability to pay attention to what's going on in and around you. The ability to pay attention cuts across all situations and contexts in your life.

Gregg and his wife, Linda Anderson Krech (Anderson Krech and Krech 2003), have developed a wonderful activity called Letting Go to help you develop mindfulness of your external environment. This activity revolves around becoming more mindful of how you touch and then let go of things. Sometimes you rush through activities like closing a drawer or putting down your cup of coffee without even realizing it. Often this rushing causes you to slam the drawer or spill your coffee. I have found that practicing the Letting Go activity periodically is a simple but effective way to remind me to slow down and pay attention to what I'm doing in the present moment.

INFORMAL MINDFULNESS ACTIVITY:
Letting Go

Devote one day in the coming week to this activity. During that day, pay attention every time your hand lets go of something. This could involve letting go of a cup or glass, a door handle, a cabinet or drawer pull, your pen, or another person's hand. Be mindful of exactly what's going on. Note how you put that glass down. Notice the movement of the doorknob when you turn it slowly and close the door gently, or when you forget and just release it from your fingers. Pay attention to the texture, weight, shape, and feel of everything you handle and then let go of. Note how paying attention to these things influences how you release them.

Think about the consequences of the way you let go of things today. Did you get a certain look from a person when you released his or her hand? Did a door or drawer slam (or not slam) when you were mindful of how you released it?

When the day is over, write down what you've learned from this activity. If you practiced this on a regular basis, how do you think being more mindful of letting go could impact your life and slow you down?

Practicing the Letting Go activity is a simple way to start practicing mindfulness by paying more attention to what's going on in your interactions with the physical world, your external environment. Paying more attention, on purpose, to your external environment will help you become more mindful of the things in it that are potential stressors for you. In the next section of the chapter, we'll look at becoming more mindful of your internal environment.

BECOMING MORE MINDFUL OF YOUR INTERNAL ENVIRONMENT

Now that you've begun to be more mindful of your external environment, it's time to shift your focus to what's going on in your mind when you're confronted by potential stressors. I'm convinced that most of our stress originates between our ears—that is, in what our minds tell us about potential stressors. Even though you can't control your internal environment (your stressful thoughts, personal scripts, scary pictures, and painful emotions), paying attention to them is crucial in learning how to manage your stress.

Rather than try to control, eliminate, or avoid the stressful thoughts, personal scripts, scary pictures, and painful emotions you have about potential stressors, I want you to start acknowledging and accepting them and sorting them out by category. With practice, you can learn how to categorize internal potential stressors according to the "traps" framework (the "thoughts are true" trap, the "thoughts are reality" trap, and so on) that you learned in chapter 3. This will help you understand how your mind works in relation to your personal stressors and how to tailor your stress management efforts toward them. For example, if most of your stress is associated with the "all thoughts are equally important" trap, you can step up your efforts to defuse this thinking when it occurs. Just by being more aware of the trap—or traps—that you most often fall into and then accepting it (or them) will facilitate your defusion efforts. The following activity, Checking the Mail, is an easy-to-use technique that will help you become more mindful of when you fall into the ten common thinking and feeling traps.

INFORMAL MINDFULNESS ACTIVITY:
Checking the Mail

Think of sorting through what your mind tells you about potential stressors the same way you would sort your mail. Imagine that your have a rack hanging from your wall that has the following ten slots:

1. The "thoughts are reality" trap

2. The "thoughts are true" trap

3. The "all thoughts are equally important" trap

4. The "thoughts are orders" trap

5. The "all thoughts are threats" trap

6. The "old, outdated thoughts and scripts" trap

7. The "scary pictures are real" trap

8. The "permanence" trap

9. The "pervasiveness" trap

10. The "personalization" trap

Take out your personal stressor journal (from chapter 3) and for each stressor look at the entry that relates to the trap you fell into regarding it. For example, in chapter 3, I used "Waiting until the last week to go Christmas shopping" as the potential stressor. The trap I fell into was the "pervasiveness" trap because I said to myself, *I'll never finish all of this shopping today and won't have time to get everybody a gift.*

Sort out all of the potential stressors according to the trap you fell into regarding them. Take a pile of the sorted potential stressors and as you read them out loud, imagine that you drop them one by one into the appropriate mail slots. Notice how many pieces of mail are in each slot. Each week look at your journal and sort your mail. As an option, you can use a real mail sorter and copies of your journal pages. Cut out the actual parts of the journal pages that relate to the traps and physically drop them in the appropriate slots.

In time, you'll notice a few things about how your mind works. You'll become more aware of what kinds of traps you fall into in response to specific potential stressors. You might notice, for example, that you fall into the "permanence" trap more frequently than others, or you might often get stuck in the "thoughts are reality" trap. You'll also become more aware of how your mind works in response to certain categories of potential stressors. For example, you might fall into the "all thoughts are threats" trap when exposed to potential stressors related to work or your boss. This might be different from the trap you fall into when confronted with potential stressors related to your partner or spouse. Eventually you'll start to recognize the traps *before* you actually fall into them. This is the final stage of awareness, the one that can help you manage your stress more effectively. When you notice that you're falling into one of the traps, you can stop and tell yourself, *Oh, I better be careful, I'm falling into the XYZ trap again. Let me step back and look at it differently.* You can then use The Whiteboard (see chapter 2) or any of the other defusion activities in this book to help you defuse from the trap. When you start noticing the traps before you actually fall into them, you're beginning to use your heightened mindfulness in a preventive fashion, as an aid to defusing stressful traps before they snap shut.

FORMAL MINDFULNESS

Formal mindfulness training involves practicing meditation. There are two main types of meditation, focused and nonfocused. Each is beneficial and will help you in your efforts to manage your stress. Each goes about things quite differently, however, so it's worth describing the differences between the two and explaining why I use both in my work with students and clients.

Focused meditation is used primarily for relaxation training and involves using a focal point to focus your attention on. Whenever you lose track of your meditation practice because your mind wanders, you redirect it to your focal point. Commonly used focal points are calming words or sounds, and inanimate objects such as candles or crystals. I'll discuss focused meditation in more detail in chapter 8.

Nonfocused meditation is often referred to as "open-focus" meditation and does not use a focal point. It is used by ACT practitioners to help people develop mindfulness. During open-focus meditation, you don't try to control your thoughts or feelings as you meditate. You simply watch them come and go.

MINDFULNESS MEDITATION

Mindfulness meditation is a form of nonfocused meditation. Mindfulness meditation fits perfectly with ACT because it does not revolve around a focal point and makes no attempt to censor incoming thoughts, sounds, and other stimuli. The purpose of mindfulness meditation from an ACT perspective is not relaxation; it is developing heightened awareness. Steve Hayes (2005) notes one of the greatest misconceptions about mindfulness meditation—that it's a way to *stop* thinking and feeling while existing in some peaceful place. He points out that when practicing mindfulness, you'll experience the same range of stressful thoughts, personal scripts, scary pictures, and painful emotions that you normally do when you're not meditating. The difference is that mindfulness meditation practice teaches you how to simply watch these things come and go while just sitting.

The "just sitting" reference is both very descriptive and very misleading. In one sense, all you do when you perform mindfulness meditation is "just sit" for an extended period. This sounds pretty simple, direct, and uncomplicated. However, unlike other times when you just sit, during mindfulness meditation you not only sit, you also pay full attention to everything going on inside and outside your body as well as in the environment around you. In other words, you're fully aware of all of the stressful thoughts, personal scripts, scary pictures, and painful emotions that enter your consciousness. You're also fully aware of the sensations going on in your body. These might be related to muscle tension, pain, breathing, or any other physiological activities that you sense. In addition, you're aware of things going on around you. You're aware of the temperature, movement of air, sounds, scents, and anything else emanating from your environment.

In addition to being aware of these internal and external stimuli, you have an accepting mind-set. You don't judge any of these stimuli. You merely note their presence and allow their passing. You don't think about their meaning, judge their quality, or wonder about where they came from or where they're going. Your experience is 100 percent focused on the here and now and your internal and external environments. When your mind wanders back to the past or forward into the future, you accept this and gently bring it back to the present. The main difference in doing this compared to what you do during focused meditation is that you don't come back to a specific focal point such as your breath. You're not trying to relax by shifting your attention to a focal point; you're trying to stay fully aware of the present moment, wherever it might take you.

The following activity, Mindfulness Meditation, provides basic guidelines for your meditation practice.

FORMAL MINDFULNESS ACTIVITY:
Mindfulness Meditation

Frequency: You need to practice mindfulness meditation at least three times a week for a couple of months to really get the hang of it and to begin to experience some of the benefits. Don't worry if you need to take a few days or a week off. You're in this for the long haul, and it's normal to experience temporary setbacks when learning a new skill.

Duration: I expose my students to mindfulness meditation gradually. I start them with five minutes for the first practice session and add five additional minutes each session until they can sit for twenty minutes. They stay at twenty minutes for a few sessions and then move to thirty minutes a session. You can use a similar step-up approach or jump right in at fifteen minutes and work up to thirty from there. Set a timer so you won't have to distract yourself by looking at your watch.

Location: As with focused meditation, it doesn't matter if you're indoors or outdoors. But wherever you choose, you should be somewhere that you will not be disturbed by other people or distractions such as the telephone, cell phone, television, or your computer. A key component of mindfulness meditation is practicing without interruption.

Posture: Sit on a cushion on the floor, or on a straight-backed chair, with your back straight and your head up and resting gently on your neck.

Practice: Sit this way for the recommended time. Pay attention to the thoughts, sensations, and feelings that come over you. Go with these wherever they take you—do not fight them. Try to endure uncomfortable physical experiences (an itch, pain, urge to move, and so on) for a while and see where this takes you. Sometimes you'll notice that these responses (like thoughts and emotions) will pass if you let them play themselves out. If you have to move, do so slowly and intentionally (think of the Letting Go activity earlier in this chapter). Continue to sit for the full time, noting what you're experiencing in an accepting, nonjudgmental way. If you catch yourself drifting to the past or present, tell yourself, *My mind is taking me out of the here and now and into the [wherever it's taking you].* If you find yourself evaluating or judging something, tell yourself, *My mind is judging or evaluating again instead of merely noting [whatever it's judging or evaluating].* As you notice things, you can label them. You can say to yourself, *I am having the feeling that...* or *I am having the thought....* You can use this self-talk to categorize anything that you're experiencing. Hayes (2005) points out that such self-talk incorporates defusion training into your meditation practice.

∞

Give yourself time to get used to mindfulness meditation. Make sure you understand how it differs from focused meditation and how it fits into your plan for learning how to manage your stress. Be patient and forgiving with yourself as you practice mindfulness meditation. It will take you time and practice to get comfortable with it, but it is time well spent. Becoming more mindful is a key component of ACT that will help you manage your stress for the rest of your life.

CHAPTER 8

Relaxation Training

When most people think of stress management, they think of relaxation training. Most students take my classes and clients come to me because they want to learn how to relax and think that's what stress management is all about. As you've seen so far, stress management is much more than relaxation training. Learning how to relax, however, is also an integral part of a comprehensive approach to stress management. A vital first step in learning how to relax is to understand the differences between the stressed state and the relaxed state.

THE STRESSED STATE

When you're stressed, your body is in a heightened state of arousal. Stress arousal is all about mobilizing energy to help you fight or flee from stressors that threaten your well-being. There are three components to this increased arousal: (1) increased nervous system activity, (2) increased muscle tension, and (3) increased negative thinking and self-talk. All three levels work together in triggering your stress response and keeping it going.

To illustrate what increased nervous system arousal means, I want you to picture how your telephone switchboard works. Somewhere in your neighborhood or the surrounding area, there's a telephone switching station where thousands of telephone lines enter from all across the country. These lines transmit messages to and from the customers whom the switching station serves. Calls and Internet messages are constantly entering and leaving the system as they are routed and rerouted along the telephone network to provide the best and fastest connection to you and the other customers.

Your nervous system works the same way. Your brain and spinal cord (the central nervous system) and the rest of your nerves (the peripheral nervous system) have millions of connections throughout your body and are constantly sending and receiving information. Some of these messages originate in your brain while others originate in other sites throughout your body, like your skin and your eyes.

Think about what happens when you try to make a telephone call or send an Internet message during peak hours or in the middle of an emergency when there are lots of other people calling and going online, flooding the switchboard with activity. Your call or message doesn't go through because your telephone line or e-mail system freezes up.

The same thing happens in your mind and body when you're stressed. Messages don't get through or are not deciphered properly. You lose your ability to focus and think clearly. You find it hard to concentrate, and sometimes, like your telephone system, your brain's circuits overload and freeze, resulting in your inability to process anything effectively.

During the stress response, your skeletal, smooth, and cardiac muscles contract and are under constant tension. Your muscles are in a constant state of readiness to fight or flee. This chronic tension causes your body to feel tight, and you find it hard to get comfortable in any position. This is called *bracing*, a state of incomplete muscle contraction and relaxation. Bracing causes muscle fatigue (and overall fatigue), pain, and eventual muscle spasms.

Increased negative thinking and self-talk mean that not only is your brain working overtime processing information, but it's also flooded with an endless procession of stressful thoughts, personal scripts, scary pictures, and painful emotions that make it hard to view situations logically. Besides having your mind race along at a breakneck pace, your negative self-talk is full of put-downs and doubts. This makes it harder to focus on the present and be fully involved in what you're doing. As you're well aware, your mind is more than capable of dwelling on the past (and what you should have done) or on the future (and what you should do) rather than on the present (and what you're currently doing).

THE RELAXED STATE

The relaxed state is the exact opposite of the stressed state. Instead of increased nervous and muscular system activity and negative thinking, your body and mind slow down. All of your major brain and body functions operate at a slower, more efficient level. Your brain and central nervous system send and receive fewer messages. The messages that are sent are communicated more efficiently. Your skeletal, smooth, and cardiac muscles loosen up, release their tension, and stop bracing. Your thoughts flow freely and easily, and you're more optimistic and feel more in control of your life.

It's impossible to be both stressed and relaxed at the same time. The two states are diametrically opposed and cannot coexist. One of the main reasons for practicing relaxation activities is to cancel out the stress response by putting your body into a relaxed state on a regular basis. These periods of relaxation can be used to recharge your body and mind and return them to a higher level of functioning.

BREATHING AND RELAXATION

Controlled, deep, even breathing facilitates relaxation. Rapid, shallow, irregular breathing disrupts relaxation. One of the main ways to know if you're stressed is the pace and depth of your breathing. If it's rapid and shallow, chances are that you're stressed. In *Peace Is Every Step* (1991), Thich Nhat Hanh, the world-renowned Buddhist monk, scholar, and author, explains that the simple practice of being more conscious of your breathing can help you relax. He found that when you practice conscious breathing, your thinking slows down, especially thoughts about past and future worries. The parts of the brain that control breathing are intimately related to the parts that control stress arousal.

If you're like most of my students and clients, you're probably only using a portion of your lungs when you breathe. Most people tend to breathe with only the top third of their lungs. To receive the stress-reducing benefits of breathing, you must learn how to get your entire lungs involved. You need to learn how to fill your lungs from the bottom up. This is called *diaphragmatic breathing*. Learning how to breathe this way takes practice, but you can master it if you spend a few moments a day practicing.

Your *diaphragm* is a large band of muscle tissue that is attached all around the lower portion of your rib cage. It separates the contents of your chest cavity (such as the lungs and heart) from the contents of your abdominal cavity (stomach, intestines, and so on). Contracting and relaxing your diaphragm affects the volume of your chest cavity and the air pressure in your lungs. If you put your hands on your belly (just below your rib cage), when you breathe in you can feel your belly push out as your diaphragm contracts and pulls downward. Some people call diaphragmatic breathing "belly breathing" because of this phenomenon. When you're stressed, the muscles in your abdomen tighten up and work against the diaphragm's natural downward push. This keeps the diaphragm from fully contracting and allowing maximum air to enter your lungs. One of the goals of practicing diaphragmatic breathing is to help you relax your belly so you can deepen your breathing and get more life-giving air into your lungs.

You can practice diaphragmatic breathing anywhere—while watching television, driving your car, at your desk at work, or while engaging in recreational activities. You don't need to do it for very long and your attention doesn't have to be exclusively focused on your breath or your lungs to reap the benefits of practicing this simple breathing technique. The following activity, Every Breath I Take, will teach you how to do diaphragmatic breathing. This activity is also contained on my relaxation CD, *Seven Weeks to Conquering Your Stress*, which can be purchased online at iTunes: www.apple.com/itunes/. Click on audiobooks and type in *Seven Weeks to Conquering Your Stress*.

RELAXATION ACTIVITY: Every Breath I Take

Focus your attention on your current breathing pattern. Make a mental note of the depth, pace, and regularity of your breathing. Visualize a picture of your lungs and your diaphragm.

Now slowly breathe in through your nose. Rest your hands on your belly, just under your ribs (unless you are driving your car—in which case, please hold on to the steering wheel). Feel your belly move out as your diaphragm pushes down against it.

As you breathe in through your nose, visualize your lungs inflating completely, starting from the bottom (the part closest to your diaphragm) and moving upward. Let your ribs expand and shoulders gently rise as your lungs inflate.

When you've filled your lungs, slowly exhale through your nose. Feel your belly push back and your diaphragm rise back into place. As you feel the movements in your belly, visualize your lungs emptying. Imagine all of the air leaving your lungs as they deflate. (Sometimes visualizing a balloon losing air or a toothpaste tube having the paste squeezed out can be helpful in understanding the emptying process.)

Continue to breathe in and out this way for a couple of minutes, paying attention to the movement of your belly and diaphragm and the visual picture of your lungs filling from the bottom up and completely emptying.

When practicing diaphragmatic breathing, don't worry about the depth and pace of your breathing, just note it. If you start to worry about it, tell yourself, *There is no need to worry about this. I am doing okay.* Don't judge your performance, just pay attention to what's going on. It'll take time and regular practice to feel fully comfortable doing diaphragmatic breathing. But in time, you'll begin to notice that you naturally take longer to fill and empty your lungs. You'll also begin to slow your breathing down. As you become more comfortable with the practice, you'll be able to switch into this type of breathing on demand. You'll find this a very valuable first line of defense when you find yourself in potentially stressful situations.

FOCUSED MEDITATION

During focused meditation, you concentrate your attention on an established focal point, and when distractions occur, you refix your attention on the focal point. While there are many forms of focused meditation, what they all have in common is the use of some form of a focal point, which can be anything. Three common focal points are objects, words, and sounds.

You can use any object as your focal point. Common objects are your breath and more visual things such as a candle flame, a crystal, or a mandala. I suggest that you use a visual image that is relaxing and conjures up peaceful, tranquil images. Try meditating to a variety of different objects to see which works best for you. I prefer a candle because the flickering flame holds my interest and is ever-changing.

Words present unlimited possibilities as focal points. I suggest that you use a relaxing word such as a color, an image, or a word that conveys peace or tranquillity. My favorite word is "Bahamas." When I use it, I can see in my mind's eye a beautiful beach where my wife and I spent an idyllic week soaking in the sun and swimming in crystal-clear, aquamarine waters. Transcendental Meditation (TM), a form of meditation popularized by the Beatles over thirty years ago, uses a special spiritual word called a *mantra*. In TM, the bestowing of a mantra by the teacher is a sacred ritual. Your personal mantra in TM is not to be shared with others. It has personal value to you alone.

Sounds can also serve as focal points, especially if they're slow and rhythmic. Some people like natural sounds—such as waves crashing on the shore or birds chirping, a heartbeat, rain, or a trickling stream—in the background to focus on. You might find pairing sounds with an object helpful. For example, sometimes when I run, I focus on the sound of my feet striking the ground. I especially like to do this in the fall when I'm running outdoors through the fallen leaves. If I'm swimming, I might focus on the sound of the air bubbles coming out of my lungs as I exhale.

You can also combine two focal points, if they reinforce each other. For example, I'll often swim focusing on my breathing and counting my strokes. I'll count the number of strokes I take with each breath. Typically I'll swim four strokes per breath while saying "1-2-3-4" to myself. At the count of four, I lift my head to breathe. While I'm not sure what swim instructors would say about the pattern, I find it very helpful when I practice meditation while swimming. You can do the same thing if you run. You can count the number of strides you take per breath instead of swimming strokes.

THE RELAXATION RESPONSE

Focused meditation induces a relaxation response that is capable of shutting down your stress response. During focused meditation, your body needs and burns less energy. It slows down and reaches a metabolic state called *hypometabolism*, which is usually reached during sleep or hibernation. Unlike these two states however, when you meditate you can achieve this deep relaxation while being awake and fully conscious. Your brain rests during meditation, and alpha-wave activity increases in intensity and frequency. *Alpha waves* are low-amplitude, slow, synchronous brain waves that are associated with a restful awake state. When you meditate, your heart and breathing rates decrease. The rate and depth of your breathing slows down due to the decreased need for oxygen associated with lowering your metabolic rate. In general, these and other functions contribute to achieving a truly relaxed state while meditating.

In his classic book on meditation, *The Relaxation Response* (1975), Dr. Herbert Benson of the Harvard Medical School describes the four conditions necessary for performing meditation: (1) a quiet environment, (2) a mental device, (3) a passive attitude, and (4) a comfortable position. Let's take a closer look at each of these now.

A quiet environment. Learning how to meditate is much easier if you practice in a quiet environment with minimal distractions. You can meditate outdoors or indoors. Many of my students and clients love to meditate on the beach, where the warm sun and the sounds of the surf provide a soothing, natural environment. Others prefer the peace and quiet of their own homes, where they can sit on the carpeted floor, draw the shades, and close the windows. It's not a good idea to meditate in an area where people will enter and leave and create distractions. If you meditate indoors, turn off your cell phone, the television, the radio, and the stereo.

A mental device. A mental device is something to use as a focal point while you meditate. As I've already mentioned, different types of mental devices include visual objects (like a candle or mandala), your breathing, a repetitive sound (such as waves or running water), a word, or a phrase. If you focus on something other than a visual object, I suggest that you close your eyes while you meditate. This will help you stay focused.

A passive attitude. A passive attitude is an accepting one. It is nonjudgmental and noncontrolling. This attitude comes into play mostly when you get distracted by thinking about the future or the past or when outside disruptions occur. When this happens, simply acknowledge the distraction and refocus on your mental device. The other part of a passive attitude is not judging your performance. Learning how to meditate takes time. You'll make mistakes and get distracted. When this happens, just accept it and keep practicing.

A comfortable position. You don't have to be a yoga master and sit in a full lotus position to meditate. Stretch a little and get comfortable before settling in to meditate. Loosen or remove any tight clothing, and make sure the room you're in has a comfortable temperature. Sit in a chair with a straight back or on the floor with your legs crossed. Do not meditate while lying down; this has a tendency to put you to sleep.

Now that you're familiar with the basic information regarding what meditation is and how it works, it's time to give it a try. The following activity, Breath Meditation, will teach you how to do breath meditation. This activity is also contained on my relaxation CD, *Seven Weeks to Conquering Your Stress,* which can be purchased online at iTunes: www.apple.com/itunes/. Click on audiobooks and type in *Seven Weeks to Conquering Your Stress.*

RELAXATION ACTIVITY: Breath Meditation

Prepare to spend twenty minutes of uninterrupted activity where you will not be disturbed by other people, the doorbell, the telephone, or anything else. This is your time to relax. You deserve this break. If your thoughts drift to other matters that need attending to, just tell yourself, *These things can wait. This is my time to relax and recharge my batteries.*

Sit comfortably on a straight-backed chair or on the floor. If you sit on a chair, keep your legs uncrossed with your feet resting comfortably on the floor and your hands resting gently on your lap. If you sit on the floor, sit on a cushion that raises your buttocks off the ground slightly while your legs are crossed comfortably and resting on the floor. Your folded hands can remain comfortably on your lap, or you can let each hand rest on a knee, palms facing up. In either position, sit up straight with your head, neck, and back in alignment.

For several breaths, focus your attention on your current breathing pattern. Make a mental note of the depth, pace, and regularity of your breathing. Slowly breathe in through your nose.

Visualize a picture of your lungs and your diaphragm. As you breathe in through your nose, visualize your lungs inflating completely, starting from the bottom (the part closest to your diaphragm, the band of muscle that separates your lungs from your abdomen) and moving upward. Feel your belly move out as your diaphragm pushes down against it. Let your ribs expand and shoulders gently rise as your lungs inflate.

When you have filled your lungs, slowly exhale through your nose. Feel your belly push back and your diaphragm rise back into place. As you feel the movements in your belly, visualize your lungs emptying. Imagine all of the air leaving your lungs as they deflate. (Sometimes visualizing a balloon losing air or a toothpaste tube having the paste squeezed out can be helpful in understanding the emptying process.)

As you continue to breathe in and out this way, try to keep your mind focused on your breathing. You might find that saying "in" as you inhale and "out" as you exhale makes it easier to keep your focus on your breathing. Say these words to yourself. Some people find that counting the seconds it takes to inhale and exhale keeps them focused on their breathing.

Whenever your thoughts stray from your breathing, don't get upset with yourself. Simply note that this happened and refocus on your breathing and the words "in" and "out" or on counting the seconds involved in your inhalations and exhalations.

Continue breathing this way for twenty minutes.

If you find that twenty minutes is too long to start with, begin with ten minutes. Each week add a couple of minutes until you can meditate for the full period. If you practice this activity at least three times a week for a couple of months, you should begin to experience some of the health and stress-reducing benefits of focused meditation. Sometimes people find it helpful to listen to the instructions for meditation and to have something such as music or natural sounds play in the background. I've recorded a twenty-minute breath meditation activity, complete with relaxing natural sounds and music, on my relaxation CD *Seven Weeks to Conquering Your Stress,* available online at iTunes (www.apple.com/itunes).

VISUALIZATION

As I discussed in the first chapter, during a stress transaction your mind judges whether or not a potential stressor is threatening. Based on a variety of factors—including the potential stressor, your personality, and your coping abilities—in a split second your mind determines the threat involved. Usually it makes good decisions about the actual threat, but sometimes it gets faked out by something that isn't really threatening. It doesn't matter, however, if the threat is not real. If your mind perceives it as real and threatening, it triggers a stress response.

A perfect example of this is watching a horror movie. Imagine you're sitting comfortably in a safe, clean, air-conditioned movie theater. You're watching a horror movie and the scene shifts to something really horrific. Think about all of the ways you might use to describe your reaction: "It made my flesh crawl," "It was hair-raising," "It made me shiver," "I had a knot in my stomach," "I got a lump in my throat." All of these statements reflect physical and emotional by-products of the stress response.

What happened was your mind perceived the action on the screen as threatening and triggered a stress response. Although there was no real threat, just viewing the scene set the processes in motion. It was so real to you that even recalling it now can have the same effects.

The same thing can happen in reverse. Your mind also has the power to trigger a relaxation response when viewing or thinking about relaxing, warming images. In other words, if you intentionally view or think about a relaxing scene, your body can switch on a relaxation response. Think about this: all you have to do to relax is imagine a relaxing scene. I like to call these relaxing visualizations "mini-vacations of the mind."

RELAXATION ACTIVITY:
Visualization: A Trip to the Beach

Visualization is best practiced by listening to a recorded visualization script. To listen to my visualization script A Trip to the Beach, go to the New Harbinger website (https//www.newharbingeronline.com/stress_less_live _more.html) and click on the link to this activity. Download it onto your own computer or MP3 player. When you are ready to listen to it, make sure you can put aside twenty minutes when you won't be disturbed by other people, the phone, the television, or any other distractions.

This relaxation visualization script contains the complete instructions for performing the visualization. The only additional thing you need to do is adopt an accepting attitude and be willing to try this activity despite any preconceived notions you might have about this type of relaxation activity.

Many of my students and clients have a hard time just letting go of the present and allowing their minds to take them on an imaginary trip to an island. They'll say things to themselves such as *How stupid, I'm not on an island, I'm just imagining it, This is the most ridiculous thing I've ever heard—letting my mind take me on an imaginary relaxing trip,* or *I feel so stupid with my eyes closed imagining I'm on an island.* If you find yourself saying such things, just accept them and get back to the visualization scene. Give it an honest effort before you judge whether or not it's something that works for you.

Creating Your Own Visualization Scripts

Different people find different scenes relaxing. My personal visualization script is based on an actual Bahamas beach scene that I experienced with my wife years ago. It was the most relaxing place I'd ever been to, and I can still recall it as if it happened yesterday instead of over thirty years ago. I also happen to love the beach. If, however, you hate walking barefoot in the sand and you view the ocean as some ominous place that contains a lot of scary sharks, my visualization script will not work for you and might actually create stress rather than relax you.

Given the unique nature of relaxing images, you might consider making your own visualization recording. There is a basic formula for creating visualization scripts (see below), and with simple, free recording programs available online, you can make your own CD if you want to. Once you've written the script and recorded it, you can play it back whenever you want to relax.

VISUALIZATION ACTIVITY:
Writing Your Personal Visualization Script

Instructions

1. **Pick a unifying, relaxing theme that your script will revolve around.** Common themes are walking on a beach, floating in a lake, and sitting in a beautiful garden or on a mountaintop.

2. **Pick specific images that are part of the scene.** The images can involve any or all sensations: sights, sounds, tastes, touches, or smells. For instance, when walking to the beach, I refer to the warm breeze, the aquamarine color of the water, and the smell of hibiscus flowers.

3. **Develop the sequence of the script.** This step involves thinking through how your script will play out. Where will it start? How will it proceed? How does it end? All scripts should start with basic instructions that prepare you to relax (loosen tight clothing, shut off the telephone ringer, and so on) and focus on your breathing for a few minutes.

4. **Write the first draft.** During this step, you actually write out the dialogue that takes you through the sequence of events in your script. When you're finished, read your script and note how long it takes. Read at a moderate to slow pace that facilitates relaxation. Don't rush your reading. To be effective, the visualization, including your introductory instructions and warm up, should last around twenty minutes.

5. **Write the final draft.** During this step, go back and add in pauses throughout the script. These pauses will help you slow down when you actually record your tape. In addition to the pauses, work in dialogue that reinforces your relaxation. Use statements such as "I am warm,

relaxed, and in control" to reinforce your ability to initiate and control your relaxation response. During the ending segment of your script, take time to slowly bring yourself back to the present state. Counting backward from ten is a good way to accomplish this.

As I mentioned earlier, one of the keys to managing stress effectively is putting your body into a relaxed state on a regular basis. This does three things for you: (1) it stops your stress response from continuing and escalating to the point where it can be physically harmful; (2) putting your body in a relaxed state reenergizes you—it allows your body to build its energy reserves back so you have resources to draw from in the future; and (3) relaxation training and ACT work beautifully together to help you manage your stress. Relaxation training relaxes your body and frees your mind so it can think more clearly and refocus your attention on your values, goals, and purposeful behavior.

Many people feel it's very difficult to find the time to relax and engage in formal relaxation activities. They say that they would like to practice the activities discussed in this chapter but are too busy with other demands on their time. In the next chapter, you'll examine your current use of time and learn ways to find the time not only to relax but also to live the life you really want to live, one that is consistent with the things you value the most.

CHAPTER 9

Finding Your Optimal Level of Stimulation and Demand

A key component of ACTing to manage your stress is finding your *optimal level of stimulation and demand*. This refers to finding the right balance of stimulating activities and demands (what some people incorrectly call stress). This is the point where you get the most out of these activities without becoming overloaded and stressed. *Stimulating activities* are things that you enjoy doing and consider fun. *Demands* are things you must do but don't particularly enjoy, such as (perhaps) cleaning the house or getting your oil changed in your car. They aren't necessarily stressors; they're just demands on your time. Since stimulating activities and demands require energy and time, I often refer to them interchangeably because they both have the potential to cause overload when you take on more than you can handle. Since you have limited quantities of energy and time, overloading yourself with too many demands or stimulating activities can transform these into stressors.

Sometimes it isn't what you do that causes stress, it's how much you take on that's the culprit. Even fun activities can become stressors if they require too much of your time and energy or if you engage in them without cutting back on other things. When you take on more than you can handle, your body and mind tell you, *I can't cope with this.* As soon as this happens, your brain initiates a stress response. I've found this to be one of the hardest stress lessons to teach. You can't assume that, just because activities are fun, you can't get overloaded and take on more than you can handle.

FINDING YOUR OPTIMAL LEVEL OF STIMULATION AND DEMAND

Finding out how much you can handle without becoming overloaded is what finding your optimal level of stimulation and demand is about. I say stimulation *and* demand because you engage in both kinds of activities every day. Your day is a mixture of things you love to do and enjoy, and things you must do that you either dislike or tolerate but don't really enjoy.

When you find your optimal level of stimulation and demand, your mind and body operate at peak efficiency and you get the most out of your potential. The only way to find your optimal level is to push yourself beyond it and then realize you've gone too far. You don't have to do this. Most people are perfectly okay operating at less than peak efficiency. If you're really serious, however, about learning how to manage your stress, you'll have to push your limits to get a sense of what you can handle.

Efficient functioning refers to your body and mind working up to their full potential. When you aren't involved in many things or don't have much responsibility, you have few demands and aren't getting much stimulation. This isn't an optimal level of demand and stimulation because you aren't operating very efficiently. At low levels of stimulation and demand, you don't ask much of your body and mind, and therefore you don't get much in return. As you begin to challenge yourself and take on more demands and a greater amount of stimulation, you become more efficient in your functioning. Quite simply, you get more out of yourself and your life when you push yourself a little.

As you take on even more demands and greater levels of stimulation, you're rewarded with even higher levels of functioning. If you keep this up, you'll eventually reach your optimal level of demand and stimulation, that point where you're pushing yourself just enough and taking on just the right amount of stimulation and demands to function at peak performance. At this point, you're busy and working hard, but the activities you're engaged in are challenges, not stressors. You're accomplishing a lot and enjoying yourself while doing so.

If, however, you continue to add more demands and stimulation, your performance begins to drop, and the same activities that were challenges and fun now become stressors. When this happens, you'll notice changes in the way you feel and in your performance. For example, you'll feel cranky, get irritated more easily, and lash out at others. You'll feel listless and tired.

You'll notice that you forget appointments, hand in work that isn't up to your standards, and constantly feel rushed to fit everything in. When this happens, you've pushed beyond your optimal level of stimulation and need to start reducing the demands on your time.

For example, imagine that you are a mom with two teenage girls. You share a house with your partner, the girls, and a dog named Pete. You've taken the past fifteen years off from your career to raise your girls and keep the house. You decide to go back to school for some retraining and to reenter the workforce. Your goal is to complete a twelve-credit certificate program in e-marketing at a local community college and have a full-time job within twelve months.

You start by enrolling in the first two courses in the e-marketing certificate program. You plan your course selection around the girls' schedules and find the classes very stimulating. You surprise yourself by doing really well in both courses. In addition to enjoying the intellectual stimulation, you find it feels good to interact with other adults and sharpen your oral and written communication skills. It's a real challenge, however, to keep up with the girls' needs, the demands of running the house, and the social life you have with your partner while completing your academic work. You manage to do this quite well, however, and reward yourself at the semester's end with a day at a local spa.

You do so well the first semester that the next term, in addition to taking two courses, you get a part-time job as a freelance e-marketer with a company that allows you to work from home. You really apply yourself during the semester. It requires more organization, hard work, and dedication than you've ever had to muster, but you find yourself excelling despite that. Your partner, though annoyed at the pile of wash in the hamper and dirty dishes in the sink, is very proud of you and amazed at how you manage to juggle everything. Your girls begin to refer to you as "supermom."

After nine months, you're doing so well you decide to move up your timetable: you get a full-time job while finishing the last two courses required to get your certificate. You've heard that these classes are very difficult and require about twice the amount of time and effort required of the other courses in the program. After two weeks on the job, you find out that the remaining two courses you need conflict with your work schedule. Your boss is very annoyed that you need to take time off of work to attend these classes. He allows you to do this, but only if you agree to come in on Saturdays to finish your work.

This really throws a monkey wrench into your personal life, as this was the time you spent playing tennis with your partner and taking your daughters shopping or to a movie. You now have only one free day left open, Sunday. Unfortunately it's no longer really free, as you must use it to do your homework, catch up on some housework, and try to fit some recreational time in with your family. After two months of this, you're ready to break down and cry. You're exhausted, your house is a mess, your family is angry with you, and you have no time for yourself. You've crossed over the line of optimal functioning, and the very same demands and stimulation that previously challenged you now cause stress.

While this is an extreme example and doesn't take into account possible things you could have done to ease the burden (getting the family to pitch in more, hire a person to clean the house, and so on), you can see how increasing demands and stimulation too drastically can transform them from challenges into stressors.

HOW DO YOU KNOW IF YOU'VE REACHED YOUR OPTIMAL LEVEL OF STIMULATION AND DEMAND?

Unfortunately there's no chart to turn to where you can look up your optimal level of stimulation and demand. I always play a trick on my students and clients regarding this. I ask them to turn to page 865 in my textbook, to the chart entitled "Optimal Level of Stimulation and Demand," and look up their optimal level based on their age, gender, height, and weight. I don't tell them that there is no page 865 or optimum level chart. Some of them get it right away, but others keep flipping back and forth, confused as to why this page is missing from the book. Eventually I tell them that the whole activity was a goof and that there is no page 865 because there could never be such a chart.

Why not? The reason there could never be such a chart is that everyone differs in how many demands and how much stimulation is optimal. The only way to find your optimal level of stimulation and demand is through experience. You must actually go beyond your optimal level to know that you have reached it. When you reach peak efficiency and then show symptoms of a decline, you've just passed your optimal level. Cut back on your demands once you reach this point and you'll get as close to optimal demand as possible.

There are two final things you need to understand about finding your optimal level of stimulation and demand. The first is that it changes over time. The second is that not all demands are of equal weight.

Remember from chapter 3 where I mentioned that the only constant in life is change? Nowhere is this more evident than in finding your optimal level of stimulation and demand. What you need at your age now to reach your optimal level of stimulation and demand will be different from what you needed ten years ago and what you will need ten, twenty, and thirty years down the road. It might be more or less, but it will change because you and your life situation will change.

In addition to this, not all demands and stimuli carry the same weight. For example, add the following three new stimuli to your life: a new hobby, a new job, and a new baby. Will they all demand the same time and energy requirements? Do they carry the same weight as any three demands you have in your life right now? I hope you can see that the new baby is a 24/7 lifetime commitment, while the new hobby and new job will put varying demands on your time and energy. If you're serious about managing your stress, it's important to think logically about the amount of time and energy required whenever you take on any new demands or stimulation.

THE NATURE OF POTENTIAL STRESSORS

Not all potential stressors are created equal. You've already seen in chapter 3 how internal potential stressors arise on their own and that they're impossible to avoid, eliminate, or control. Therefore let's focus our attention on external potential stressors in this section. There are really three different types of external potential stressors. For simplicity's sake we'll call them types 1, 2, and 3.

Type 1 external potential stressors are those that you can anticipate and avoid. In other words, you can see them coming and you can do something about them. They're typically potential stressors that you know about in advance and therefore have time to work on. For instance, if you know that driving in the snow makes you nervous, you can choose not to drive when it's snowing. You can stay home, use mass transportation, or have someone else drive you where you need to go.

Type 2 external potential stressors are those that you can anticipate but can't avoid. These stressors require different coping strategies because you can't avoid them. Type 2 potential stressors are usually beyond your ability to control without suffering negative consequences. An example of this kind of stressor is making a presentation at work. You're generally stressed by doing any kind of public speaking but can't avoid this job-related responsibility without suffering a career setback. While this type of stressor is foreseeable, you can't avoid or control it. There are ways to make it less stressful, but it differs from type 1 stressors because it cannot be avoided or controlled.

Type 3 potential stressors are those that you don't see coming, and you can't avoid or control them. These are the stressors that catch you completely off guard. An example of this type of stressor is your company moving to another state. Your boss offers to take you and to pay for your relocation expenses. You had no idea this was going to happen and can't do anything about it. You could neither foresee this happening nor control it when it did.

Of the three types of external potential stressors, you have the least control over managing type 3. Over the years, I've found that people seem to have the hardest time dealing with type 3 potential stressors because of their inability to control them. I find this interesting because it seems to me that, since you have the least control over type 3 stressors, they should be the *easiest* to accept and manage. Despite your best intentions and efforts to prevent them from happening, they still occur. Since you have the least ability to control these, you need to learn how to accept them and move on. Practicing the acceptance and willingness activities described in chapter 3 can help you learn how to do this. I think it's much more productive to focus your efforts on managing the stressors you have some degree of control over rather than ruminating over those that are beyond your ability to control.

Of course this is much harder to do when unexpected catastrophic events occur, such as losing everything to Hurricane Katrina or losing your health insurance unexpectedly when your employer goes out of business. In these cases, you might need the help of a social service provider and a licensed therapist to accept what happened and begin to move forward again.

THE TRIPLE A'S OF COPING

I've developed a very simple but effective way to reduce stressors called the "triple A's of coping." The triple A's are abolish, avoid, and alter. *Abolish* means completely eliminating potential stressors. *Avoid* refers to minimizing your exposure to them. *Alter* means somehow changing the way you are exposed to the potential stressor.

Let's use the triple A's to work through how to deal with a typical type 1 potential stressor, rush-hour traffic. Imagine that your commute to work in the morning is a major source of stress for you. You report to work at 9:00 a.m., five days a week. Driving to work at this time of day puts you right in the middle of rush-hour traffic.

Abolish. You could abolish this stressor by just quitting your job. If you do this, you have no job and therefore no commute. Problem solved! Realistically, however, you want and need this job, so you decide to focus on abolishing your commute. There are many ways to do this. You can change where you live. You can either move to the same town where you work or move very close (within five miles) so your commute is negligible. You weigh both options, speak to your spouse about this, and decide that this isn't the best thing to do. You could also change your work hours. If you report to work earlier or later in the day on those five weekdays, you won't be exposed to the same volume of traffic. Your company has flex hours, so you decide to speak to your boss about rearranging your schedule. Your boss tells you that as long as you work during the company's core hours (10:00 a.m. – 3:00 p.m.) and put in eight hours a day, you can work anytime during the hours of 7:00 a.m. – 7:00 p.m. You talk this over with your spouse and decide that you might consider this next year, but right now it's important for you to be home in the morning to help get your kids ready for school.

Avoid. Since you can't abolish your commute, you shift to the second A, avoid. Using this strategy, you don't completely eliminate the stressor—you simply minimize the number of times you're exposed to it. The idea is that if you can cut your exposure to the stressor by a certain percentage, you can cut the stress associated by that same percentage. For example, if you could cut your exposure to a stressor by 50 percent, you could cut 50 percent of the stress associated with it. This isn't as good as completely eliminating it, but it's 50 percent better than 100 percent exposure. Your company has two options for helping you: part-time telecommuting and working four days instead of five. You talk to your boss about these two options. Your boss explains that you can telecommute two days a week by working at home. This would cut 50 percent of your commuting stress. He explains further, however, that to do this you must have a home office where you can set up a home computer and a dedicated telephone line to receive and send faxes. You'll also have to buy your own home computer and fax machine, since your work computer is a desktop, not a laptop you can take back and forth with you, and the company is not able to buy a second computer or a fax machine for you. They'll pay for the dedicated telephone line, but you must buy the equipment. You don't have the money for this equipment or any additional space to set up a private home office, so you decide against this option.

Your boss explains that you can change to a four-day workweek. This will avoid one day of commuting and reduce your stress by 20 percent. You would report to work on Mondays through Thursdays from either 7:00 a.m. – 5:00 p.m. or 9:00 a.m. – 7:00 p.m. You talk this over with your spouse and decide that working four 10-hour days in a row to avoid the traffic one day a week isn't worth it. You move on to the final A, alter.

Alter. You can use the third A, alter, to somehow change the stressor or your exposure to it. There are several ways to alter the actual experience of commuting. You're still going to be exposed to the same commute, for the same number of days each week, but you'll be exposed to it differently. If you can alter the way in which you're exposed to the commute, you can defuse it as a stressor.

You list all of your options on a legal pad. Carpooling is one way to alter your exposure to your commute. By being a passenger in a carpool, you can sit back, read the paper, or take a nap during the ride to work. Unfortunately you find the thought of being a passenger with someone else driving is more stressful than driving yourself. You check out the company's vanpool schedule and costs, and you find that it's expensive and inconvenient. To take advantage of this, you'd have to drive to a location other than your home to meet the vanpool.

You think about trying a different route to work. Other than the highway, your usual route, there is a back road that takes a little longer but doesn't have much traffic. The change of scenery might be enough to defuse the commute as a stressor. You do this for a week and decide that this is something that works. The slightly longer ride is definitely offset by the slower pace and interesting scenery. You also decide to install a jack in your car for your MP3 player and listen to comedy or peaceful music while driving. You find that even when traffic slows, your music is relaxing and it helps ease your tension.

You also decide to start listening to audiobooks while driving. You like to read, so you find the idea of listening to someone read your favorite books appealing. You start listening to Shakespeare during your commute.

Now it's your turn. Use your stressor journal from chapter 3 to find a type 1 stressor and work through the following activity, Reducing Stressors with the Triple A's. It will help you apply this technique to one of your own personal stressors.

ASSESSMENT ACTIVITY:
Reducing Stressors with the Triple A's

Instructions

1. Look through your stressor journal. Pick a type 1 stressor that you think can be reduced using the triple A's technique.

2. Work through each A by listing as many possible ideas as you can think of. Don't worry about how crazy the idea might seem, just put it down. The more ideas, the better.

3. Go back and pare down the ideas for each A to four or five. Investigate each idea for each A completely. Find as much data as possible regarding your ideas to abolish, avoid, or alter the stressor.

4. Decide on the best possible A and feasible ideas to implement it. Implement the strategy and give it a two-month trial to see if it works. At the end of two months, evaluate whether the A worked and which, if any, of your implementation strategies need to be improved.

5. Make any necessary adjustments and repeat step 4 in two more months.

Go back to your stressor journal and look for additional stressors that you might manage using this simple technique. Try abolishing some of these stressors that are linked to timelines. These are the easiest to abolish. For example, if one of your stressors is linked to a position whose term is about to expire (committee chairperson, coach, manager, den mother, or others), let it happen. Use the end of the term as a time to abolish the stressor.

While the triple A's of coping offer a very easy framework for you to use to reduce your external potential stressors, they don't work against all types of stressors under all conditions. In particular, this technique doesn't work with internal potential stressors. That's okay—you have plenty of other tools to use for those.

DOES ANYBODY REALLY KNOW WHAT TIME IT IS?

The meaning of time is relative. I know, I know, this sounds like typical philosophical drivel from a professor sitting somewhere in an ivory tower. I apologize for starting this section with such an esoteric statement, but it really is consistent with an ACT view of the world. Time means different things to different people. It also means different things to different cultures and is influenced by geography, climate, and a host of other factors.

The concept of time, and instruments for measuring it, did not exist before humans created them. Think of sundials, clocks, watches, calendars, time zones (Eastern Standard and so on), and adjustments to time zones such as Daylight Savings Time. All of these creations originated with the human need to organize and segment time so work could get done. That's what time is really about, segmenting the day to accommodate work. Whether you're plowing fields or figuring out when the opening bell on Wall Street should ring, organizing and segmenting time is crucial in making the wheels of the work world roll smoothly. I'll use two different scenarios to illustrate this.

Imagine you're in a committed relationship and have two kids. Both of your children are in middle school and involved in after-school activities. You and your partner work in professional jobs and commute thirty minutes each way. Think about your typical day. It's filled with appointments for you and your partner at work. You have meetings, reports due, presentations in progress, and deadlines to meet. Your kids don't drive, so you and your partner juggle schedules to ensure that one of you is always there to drop off and pick up the kids. Dinner is built around juggling schedules and other priorities. On top of this, your parents, who live in town, are aging and need help doing chores and getting to doctors' appointments. You're conscious of every minute of every day. You'd be lost without your cell phone, laptop, BlackBerry, and multiple calendars, appointment books, and sticky notes scattered all over your house and office. What does time mean to you?

Now let's shift gears. Imagine that just you and your partner are on a vacation on an island off the coast of Central America. You're in the tropics: it's warm, moist, sunny. The only people around are the staff at your resort hideaway, and they're laid-back and accommodating. Your kids and parents are in safe hands, and it's just you and your partner—alone, on an island, with nowhere to go and nothing to do. You've left your laptop, cell phone, BlackBerry, and watch at home. Your hut has no television. You have no work to do and no reason to get up or go to bed at specific times. It'll take you a day or two to adjust, but assuming that you want to be on this vacation alone with your partner and that you like the solitude of an island, you'll probably stop caring about time after the initial adjustment period. You might even find that time stands still when you have nothing to do and nowhere to go. The only thing that will let you know what time it is will be the position of the sun and the meal schedule at the resort. What does time mean to you in this context?

Does Anybody Really Care?

Why do you care about time? If you're like most of my clients and students, the reason you care about time is that you have places to go and things to do. Time matters when you have goals that need to be met. In fact, I'll go out on a limb and say that's the only reason time matters. If you have no job, no commitments to others, and no formal responsibilities, why would you care about time? Okay, I forgot that you'll need to know when your favorite television programs are on. Seriously, when you think about why time is important, it takes you back to your values and goals.

Time gives you the structure to meet your goals. When you have goals, you can use your wonderful mind to think ahead and plan.

Keeping Track of Your Time

A time journal can help you get a better sense of how you use your time and whether or not it helps you meet your goals. Just like your stressor journal provides valuable information regarding your potential stressors, a time journal will give you a visual picture of how you spend your time. As you can see, the two do go together and keeping both journals will allow you to see the interaction between your use of time and your stressors. I've had countless students and clients say things like "When I first started keeping this time journal, it was a real pain in the neck. But now after keeping it for two months, I can see the value. It's one thing to think about how you use your time, but it's an entirely different thing to see it on paper. I was amazed at how many hours I spent doing certain things like watching television or surfing the Web." The following activity, My Personal Time Journal, will help you get a better picture of how you actually use your time and whether you use it efficiently.

ASSESSMENT ACTIVITY:
My Personal Time Journal

Starting today, keep a journal of your use of time. Keep the journal every day for at least four weeks. You can keep this in whatever format you desire: electronic, lined paper, bound journal, and so on. You can fill in the categories whenever it's convenient for you—as they occur, at the end of the day, and so on. I recommend that you don't let more than a day pass without recording the prior day's use of time. This will keep the details of it from blurring.

Each line in your journal represents one 30-minute segment of your day. Put the day and the date at the top of each page or 24-hour period. (See the sample below.) Put the time at the beginning of each line. I suggest you start at 12:00 midnight and add thirty minutes to that for the next line and each subsequent line (12:30 a.m., 1:00 a.m., 1:30 a.m., and so on). At the end of each line, make two columns (yes and no columns). These refer to whether you used that time segment efficiently (yes) or inefficiently (no).

Every day you keep the journal, be sure to fill in all forty-eight lines (twenty-four 30-minute segments). On each line, list the activities you engaged in during that period (sleeping, getting ready for work, waiting for the kids' school bus, and so on). If you're engaged in continuous activity (like sleeping) for several 30-minute segments, use ditto marks on the lines following your initial notation of the activity. At the end of the line, check off whether or not you used the time efficiently.

Spend ten to fifteen minutes at the end of each of the four weeks examining your time journals and assessing where you used your time efficiently and inefficiently. Look for patterns and trends in your use of time.

MY PERSONAL TIME JOURNAL: A SAMPLE

(starting at 5:00 a.m. for illustration purposes):

Day/Date

Saturday, August 5, 2009

Time	Activity	Efficient Use of Time	
		Yes	**No**
5:00 a.m.	*sleeping*	√	
5:30 a.m.	*sleeping*	√	
6:00 a.m.	*woke up, brushed teeth*	√	
6:30 a.m.	*rode exercise bike and watched news*	√	
7:00 a.m.	*ate breakfast and read newspaper*	√	
7:30 a.m.	*showered*	√	
8:00 a.m.	*played video games*		√
8:30 a.m.	*played video games*		√

You would continue the log like this for the rest of the day. While it may seem tedious to keep this journal, you'll find that it's one thing to *think about* how you use your time and another thing to actually *see it* on paper. You'll be surprised by the actual chunks of time you devote to certain activities. These seem to jump off the page at you. Spend ten to fifteen minutes at the end of the week examining your time journals and assessing where you used time efficiently and inefficiently. These will help you decide which activities contribute to the efficient use of your time and which rob you of precious time and make it hard to reach your goals.

I'd just like to mention why I use the word "efficient" instead of "productive" when assessing how you use your time. "Efficient" to me means your time was spent in a helpful way. It helped you meet your goals. If you're like most people I work with, you probably have some stressful thoughts, personal scripts, scary pictures, and painful emotions related to thinking that you *must* be productive 24/7, fifty-two weeks a year. You probably experience a little guilt or anxiety when you just get lazy or goof off. So much of this kind of thinking is related to accepting a nose-to-the-grindstone cultural ethic that might not work for you.

For example, sometimes I like to just sit by the side of my pool with a gin and tonic and watch the clouds roll by. If I'm really feeling decadent, I'll do this while floating in a tube in my pool. If my goal is to relax, I think spending an hour doing this is fun and that it's an efficient use of my time. Was this a "productive" use of my time? Did I produce anything? The answer is no. I was simply relaxing. I think spending time relaxing and having fun can be very efficient uses of your time, as long as they don't interfere with meeting your goals. In fact, relaxing and taking breaks can facilitate meeting other goals because they allow you to step away from what you're doing and come back refreshed and ready to see the task through.

One word of caution, however: if your goals are set too high and in order to meet them you must be productive 24/7, you need to reset your goals, give yourself more time to accomplish them, and build in a little fun time into your schedule.

TIME AND THE NATURE OF PLANNING

In his book *The Worry Trap* (2007), Chad LeJeune describes a key component of planning: making sequential lists of actions you need to take. Because your mind has the ability to use information from the past to extrapolate into the future, it excels at planning. When you plan, you imagine how things will play out if you follow a certain course of action. You take into account how much time you think you'll need to complete your plans, and you develop a course of action with a timeline. Your mind has the ability to anticipate problems that might crop up and things that could go wrong with your plan. This isn't a problem as long as these concerns aren't excessive (such as wanting to control the future) and are based on solid evidence and not speculation.

Unfortunately your mind can ruminate endlessly about past mistakes and use these as evidence for things that could possibly go wrong in the future. In other words, by ruminating on past problems and projecting them onto your current plans even if there isn't a shred of evidence to support this, your mind sabotages your planning process. When this happens, you fall into the "worry trap." Getting out of the worry trap involves accepting the things you can't control about your plan; coexisting with the stressful thoughts, personal scripts, painful emotions, and scary pictures that come along for the ride; and taking valued action to meet your goal.

Rumination and worry are tremendous time wasters. I have met hundreds of students and clients who literally get stuck on their plans because of excessive worry and rumination over past problems and mistakes. It's as if they're carrying around a large sack that weighs them down and makes forward progress difficult. The following defusion activity, Just Drop It, can help you stop wasting time and leave your worries behind.

DEFUSION ACTIVITY: Just Drop It

Take one of the goals you set for yourself in chapter 4 and look at the timeline you attached to the objectives. Remember, a measurable objective answers this question: Who will do how much of what by when? If you did not set a time frame for accomplishing the objective, do it now. Try to choose an objective that's especially challenging and that you worry about.

Now I want you to list all of the things that you can't control regarding meeting this objective. Be creative—don't sell this list short.

Add to this list all of the things you screwed up in the past when you tried to meet a similar objective and timeline. It doesn't have to be the exact same goal or objective, just something similar. For example, if you were trying to save money for a down payment on a house in the past and your current objective is saving money for a new car, you can ruminate on how things went with the house.

After you have both lists, I want you to put these in a sack, duffle bag, laundry bag, or pillowcase along with about twenty pounds of some other material (sand, books, or whatever). Now sling this bag over your shoulder and walk around with it for five minutes.

As you walk, I want you to visualize all of the baggage that the contents of the sack represent. These are all of the things you worry about and can't control regarding this current objective you're working on. Keep thinking about these things for the full five minutes.

After five minutes, I want you to say to yourself, *I don't need to let these things weigh me down anymore. I can just drop the sack anytime I want. These things will still be there, in my sack, but they don't have to slow me down as I work toward meeting this objective.*

Continue to repeat this to yourself for a few more minutes while carrying the sack. Then carefully drop the sack and slide it into a corner.

Now walk around for a couple of more minutes focusing on what you need to do next to get started on your plan to meet your goal. As you walk and focus on this, make sure to pass the sack a few times and note that it's still there.

Hopefully this activity will help you see that your fears and worries don't have to weigh you down and keep you from moving forward. You can coexist with your fears and worries as you plan for the future and take valued action. They'll still be there, out of the way in the corner, but they won't weigh you down anymore.

AN ACT MODEL OF TIME MANAGEMENT

Time management is an issue only when you feel that you don't have the time to meet all of your goals and objectives, or if you feel that you're wasting time and want to use it more efficiently. Years ago I developed a model for time management called the "ACT model." Little did I know that it would come to have the same letters in it as acceptance and commitment therapy!

The ACT model is an approach to time management that revolves around making priority lists of things that you need or like to accomplish during any given day. Each activity is assigned a different priority status and is acted upon based on its priority. A stands for things that "absolutely" must get done today. C relates to things that "could" get done and T refers to activities that you'll "try" to do. Activities with the highest priority (A) are acted on first. Activities of lesser priority (C and T) are acted upon only after A activities are finished. Now let's take a closer look at using the ACT model.

A-list activities are things that *absolutely* must get done today or you'll suffer unacceptable consequences. These are things that in your estimation you can't put off until tomorrow. A-list activities are totally subjective: only you can determine what these activities are. You can include things such as paying bills, completing work assignments, driving the kids to school, meditating for thirty minutes, or whatever else you choose. The key criteria for inclusion is that if you don't accomplish the activity, you'll suffer unacceptable (however you define "unacceptable") consequences.

C-list activities are things that *could* get done when you finish your A-list tasks. For example, a work project that is due next month is a C-list activity. Although you'd like to work on it, you can put it off until tomorrow and not suffer any negative consequences today if you have a more important project that must get finished by the end of the day.

T-list activities are things you would like to *try* to do if you complete all of your A-list and C-list tasks. Things like shopping for a new outfit or organizing your photos on the Internet might be examples of T-list activities. The following time management activity, Getting Organized, ties together the key elements of the model.

TIME MANAGEMENT ACTIVITY: Getting Organized

Instructions

1. Take out a piece of paper and divide it into three columns. Label the columns A-list, C-list, and T-list.

2. In the A-list column, write all of the things that you absolutely must complete tomorrow.

3. In the C-list column, write all of the things that you could work on once you finish your A-list activities.

4. In the T-list column, write all of the things that you'd like to try to do once you finish your A-list and some of your C-list activities.

5. Tomorrow cross off the individual activities as you complete them.

A good time to make up your ACT priority lists is at the end of the day. You can start by assessing the current day's remaining C- and T-list activities. Combine these with the next day's new activities to come up with your A-list tasks for tomorrow.

You don't need to spend a lot of money on gadgets to post your A-list. I use a sticky note that I put on my computer screen. Other people prefer color-coded schedule books, notebook computers, or electronic gadgets to keep track of their lists.

You can work through your A-list any way you want. Some people like attacking the more difficult items first. In this way, they work on the most difficult problems when they're the freshest and have the most energy. Others like to knock off several smaller tasks first to get a sense of accomplishment right off the bat. There is no correct way to do it. Whatever works for you is the best way to do it.

The most important thing to remember about a priority system such as this is to finish your A-list before moving on to your C- or T-lists. It's very tempting to stop doing what you have to do to pursue something else that is more fun or less important. This invariably leads to stress, however, as your A-list deadlines get closer and you haven't made the necessary progress toward meeting them. This is when you find yourself taking unfinished work home or staying up late to accomplish things that could have been finished on time. Doing this brings you past your optimal level of demands for the day and creates stress because you can't cope with the pressure.

THE POWER OF FINDING YOUR OPTIMAL LEVEL OF STIMULATION AND DEMAND

As you learned in this chapter, a key component of managing your stress is finding your optimal level of stimulation and demand. When you find the right balance of stimulating activities and demands for yourself, you feel energized and optimistic. You begin to look forward to each day because you know that the activities you're involved in will move you closer to achieving your goals while staying true to your values. Finding your optimal level of demand and stimulation is uplifting because it helps you stay true to who you are as a person. It allows you to take on new responsibilities and challenges and let go of the demands on your time and your energy that bring you down and interfere with doing what you need to do to meet your goals.

☙❧

In the next chapter, you'll learn how assertiveness, nonassertiveness, and aggressiveness factor into finding your optimal level of stimulation and demand. You'll see how many people get overloaded and sidetracked in their quest to meet their goals by their inability to say no and resist the demands of others.

CHAPTER 10

Assertiveness, Aggressiveness, Nonassertiveness, and Stress

In the last chapter, you learned how to find your optimal level of stimulation and demand. This is an invaluable step in ACTing to manage your stress. Once you've established your optimal level, you've got to take steps to reduce unwanted demands and stimulation. Doing this involves asserting yourself and being more proactive in setting the agenda for your life rather than doing what others want or expect you to do. This might prove difficult for you if your stressful thoughts, personal scripts, scary pictures, and painful emotions related to assertiveness keep you stuck in unhelpful behavior patterns created years ago.

I was stuck in such a pattern for about thirty years. I grew up learning that I should be a "nice boy," not cause trouble for others, and attempt to please others as much as possible. This was compounded by the fact that my older brother was not such a nice boy and caused my parents incredible grief and problems. I felt that, given the pain and suffering he caused them, I had to be extra nice. My primary orientation was to please others and be nice rather than take care of my own needs. In my childhood, teen, and young adult years, I was never taught the difference between assertiveness and aggressiveness; I always thought that they were the same thing. Aggressiveness was always viewed negatively in my family, and being "pushy" was considered one of the worst personality attributes to have. It wasn't until I was in my mid-thirties that I fully understood the difference between assertiveness and aggressiveness, and I began to realize how being nonassertive had really impacted my life negatively. I hope this chapter can spare you from what I had to suffer through.

AGGRESSIVENESS, ASSERTIVENESS, AND NONASSERTIVENESS DEFINED

Assertiveness is pursuing your wants and needs without infringing on the rights of others to pursue theirs. Assertiveness assumes that you know who you are and what you want and need to be happy and live a purposeful life. To be assertive, you must be in touch with your values and have goals and aspirations. Being assertive is based on mutual respect and democracy in relationships. The key to acting assertively is the way in which you go about meeting your wants and needs. When you behave assertively, you respect the rights of others when meeting your needs. Assertiveness is often thought of as being synonymous with aggressiveness, and many people shy away from being assertive because they fear that others will label them as aggressive if they stand up for their rights. The major difference between assertiveness and aggressiveness is the manner in which you meet your needs.

Aggressiveness is pursuing your needs and wants without any regard to how this affects the rights of others. Often aggressive people get their needs met at the expense of others. While aggressive and assertive people are similar in that they both know who they are and what they need and want, the aggressive person goes out and gets these things without regard for how their actions affect other people. This is a potentially much more stressful approach to getting your needs met, because you often create enemies and fail to cultivate social support when you trample on others's rights in order to get your needs met.

Nonassertiveness is failing to pursue your needs and wants while allowing others to meet theirs at your expense. When you are nonassertive, you don't stand up for your rights and you allow others to take advantage of you. Lack of assertiveness is a major reason for becoming overburdened with commitments and demands on your time and energy that interfere with doing what you want or need to do. In addition, when you're nonassertive, resentment builds up inside of you until it spills over into outright self-loathing or hostility toward others.

When you behave in a nonassertive way, it's often aimed at trying to avoid conflict. You'll say yes to doing things that you really don't want to do. This temporarily relieves the guilt you feel for wanting to say no in the first place. Unfortunately, however, when you do this, you get trapped into doing things that overburden you and create stress. When this happens, you begin to feel miserable because you've lost control of your time and your life.

Sometimes putting the needs of others ahead of your own is inevitable. For example, if you're a parent you often put the needs of your children ahead of your own. If you're caring for your sick parents, your needs often take a backseat to theirs. There are countless examples of times when your service to others takes precedence over meeting your own personal needs. In most cases, you do this willingly and it reflects your values. In addition, the people you serve don't have ulterior motives, aren't manipulating you, and are truly in need of your help. Willingly putting your own needs on the back burner while you serve others such as your children or your elderly parents shouldn't be confused with a lack of assertiveness.

YOUR ASSERTIVENESS RIGHTS

Now that you understand the differences among assertiveness, aggressiveness, and nonassertiveness, I'll assume that you want to start behaving more assertively. Remember, you can do this without denying others the same thing. I do have one warning, however: some of the people who know you won't understand the change. They'll perceive you as being more aggressive, and it'll take them a while to get used to the new you. This is *their* problem, not yours. The following assertiveness rights will help you put the differences among assertiveness, aggressiveness, and nonassertiveness into the proper perspective:

- ᘒ You don't have to justify your behavior.

- ᘒ You have the right to change your mind.

- ᘒ You have the right to say, "I don't care."

- ᘒ You have the right to agree to disagree.

- ᘒ You have the right to not have to solve other people's problems.

- ᘒ You have the right to say no.

Let's take a closer look at each of these rights.

You don't have to justify your behavior. You are an adult. You're protected by the laws of your country. You're free to make up your own mind. You can do anything you want (within legal limitations, of course) without having to justify it or ask permission. The only thing you have to do is to be willing to live with the consequences of your behavior.

You have the right to change your mind. I can't tell you how many people I've worked with grew up learning that changing their minds was a sign of immaturity or instability. If you've read this book, you realize that resetting goals and changing plans is a rational and logical way to behave. Sometimes things turn out differently than you expected when you set your goals and began to take action. There's nothing wrong with changing your mind and your plans if, after a reasonable amount of time, things don't turn out the way you expected them to turn out.

You have the right to say, "I don't care." I know this sounds pretty insensitive, but you don't have to care about everything, everyone, and every problem. Trust me, there are lots of other people out there who care about the things that you couldn't care less about. If something doesn't resonate within you, forcing yourself to care about it won't work. While it seems nice to care about everything and everyone (especially those who seem to care about you), it's okay not to. Remember, acting assertively concerning the things you do care about doesn't deny others the right to care about these other things.

You have the right to agree to disagree. I can't even begin to tell you how much stress I see in my students and clients caused by arguing over who's right or wrong regarding some issue. I see countless entries in stressor journals about getting into arguments and fights over trying to convince others to accept their positions. It's a major avoidable potential stressor. It's not being aggressive or rude to simply say, "I understand your position, but I do not share it or agree with it." If you really want to be assertive and get them to stop pestering you, follow that sentence with "...and I really don't care much about that issue." You don't have to accept another person's opinion as your own if you don't share it. Very few issues can be explained just one way. Unless you're talking about a scientific fact, most of the positions people want you to agree with are pretty subjective and based on their opinions. Even the best scientific research is usually only 90 to 99 percent reliable.

You have the right to not have to solve other people's problems. Wow, talk about insensitive, how could I possibly say this? How many times do you get caught in the middle of other people's dramas because you are such a "nice" person? How often does being nonassertive cause you to get sucked into feeling responsible for solving other people's problems? If you're like most of my students and clients, this probably happens a lot. People make all kinds of stupid decisions and mistakes. Many of the problems this creates aren't easily solved, if they can be fixed at all. You aren't their therapist. You bought this book because you're having your own problems. If you spend most of your time feeling responsible for everyone else, you won't have enough time to care for yourself and meet your own goals. You have to be very selective about whom you will help and how involved you get if you don't want to get overloaded and move beyond your optimal level of demand. There's a fine line here. Only you can decide when to cross it. Be careful, because many of the problems others bring to your doorstep cannot be solved by you; they can be solved only by the others themselves.

You have the right to say no. There's no absolute legal, moral, or ethical reason that forces you to say yes to something you don't want to do. You can say no to anything you want to without having to justify it and without having to have a good reason, or any reason, other than you simply don't want to do it. Obviously the closer you are to the person asking you to do something, the more compelled you'll feel to offer a reason, but the bottom line is that you don't have to supply one if you don't want to.

Saying no is not always easy, but it's essential if you're to be assertive and you want to reduce your stress. Here's a simple activity called How to Say No to help you get better at saying no when you really mean it.

ASSERTIVENESS ACTIVITY: How to Say No

Instructions

1. Look for opportunities during the coming week to say no to someone regarding a request they make of you. Start with telephone solicitations if the following in-person guidelines are too threatening. (If you start with telephone solicitations, skip the next three steps.)

2. Face the other person from a normal distance (three to five feet). If you're farther away than this, you'll appear timid and they won't take you seriously. If you're too close, you will intimidate them and come off as being aggressive.

3. Stand proudly with your head up, shoulders squared, and your body relaxed. Facing people sidesaddle, with your shoulder pointing at them instead of your torso, is less effective.

4. Look the other person directly in the eye. If you avoid eye contact, you're more likely to cave in.

5. Speak slowly, clearly, firmly, and at a volume that can be heard.

6. Just say "no" or "no, thank you." You don't need to clarify or explain why you choose not to do what they want you to do.

7. Be prepared to repeat your message. Sometimes people don't take the first no as an answer. Don't give in. Saying no gets easier with practice.

8. If the person you're saying no to is someone who you feel deserves an explanation regarding why you're declining, here are a few tips for doing this:

    ∾ Thank the person for the offer. Say something like, "Thank you so much for thinking of me and asking me to do this, but no thanks. I'm not interested."

    ∾ Express appreciation. Use a statement such as "I really appreciate the offer, but no thanks. I'm not interested."

    ∾ Affirm your friendship: "You're my best friend and I really love you, but no thanks. I'm not interested in doing this at all."

Give yourself a few months to get used to asserting yourself by saying no. It'll be difficult at first, but it gets easier with practice. If you don't stop saying yes to everyone else's demands, you'll never reach your optimal level of demand and stimulation.

AN ACT VIEW OF ASSERTIVENESS

Many of the demands on your time and energy revolve around other people's needs. All kinds of people count on you to do things for them every day. I'm always amazed when I examine the time and stressor journals of my students and clients and see just how much of their stress is caused by this. As an objective observer without any personal connections to these other people making the demands, it's easier for me to step back and objectively look at the effects that serving them has on my students and clients. It's much harder for you to look at all you do for others and to assess whether or not it's worth it. Periodically look through your time and stressor journals and see how much of your stress is associated with being nonassertive and spending too much time doing what others want and need instead of working toward meeting your goals.

Taking an ACT approach with this will help put it into perspective for you. Remember, acceptance and commitment therapy helps you get unstuck when your psychological inflexibility keeps you from making progress toward meeting your values-based goals. Getting unstuck often revolves around assessing whether or not the stressful thoughts, personal scripts, scary pictures, and painful emotions are helpful in trying to meet your goals. While it's important and even noble to help others, there is a threshold for this. You reach a point where you can serve others only at your own expense—and then you get stuck.

Many of your problems with being more assertive revolve around illogical stressful thoughts, outdated personal scripts, scary pictures, and painful emotions that were created in your childhood and youth. I remember my mother telling me a thousand illogical shoulds, oughts, and musts regarding my behavior. See if any of these sound familiar to you: "You should try to be nice to everybody," "You have to listen to your elders," "You must finish everything on your plate because people are starving in Africa," "You must come with us to ABC," "You can't do XYZ," "Be nice to Aunt So-and-So, even if she's not nice to you," "You must not be too pushy, because people won't like you," or "Be a nice boy and do that for me [or a hundred other adults]."

I can still see all of these scenes in my mind's eye, and even fifty years later, I feel the anger, fear, guilt, shame, and confusion associated with them. I can see myself as the helpless little boy being dragged to places I didn't want to go, forced to do things I didn't want to do (like being forced to kiss a million wrinkly old faces of my parents' friends and relatives), and live a life I didn't choose for myself. I still carry all of this around in that sack with my other outdated personal scripts and scary pictures, but I've learned to drop the sack and leave it in the corner most of the time.

The following two defusion activities can help you step back and begin to view your assertiveness-related scripts from a different perspective.

DEFUSION ACTIVITY: Silly, Outdated Scripts

Instructions

1. Go back and look through the scrapbook you put together in chapter 2.

2. Pull out the photos and other items that are associated with assertiveness-related stressful thoughts, personal scripts, painful emotions, and scary pictures that you developed when they occurred years ago. If you can't find any in your scrapbook, go back to other photo albums that have pictures of you with people who were inappropriate role models regarding how to be assertive.

3. Make copies of each photo or other items with a copy machine. If possible, enlarge the faces of the people in these photos.

4. Take one picture and have fun making the person look as silly as you can. Draw mustaches, beards, crazy glasses, dangly earrings, or anything else you want on the photos to make the person look as silly as possible.

5. Now do this with several of the pictures.

6. Write a label that reads "Silly Assertiveness Photos" on a large manila envelope.

7. As you slowly drop each picture into the envelope, say to yourself: *This silly fool is no longer going to control how I deal with things that I no longer want to do with my life. From now on, [he or she] will stay in this envelope in the back of my mind as I learn new ways to act more assertively.*

DEFUSION ACTIVITY: Funny Voices

Instructions

1. Go back to the enlarged copies of the photos you made in the last activity (Silly Outdated Scripts) and choose five images to work with.

2. Take one picture and, instead of making the picture look silly, match it up to one of your favorite cartoon characters. Choose a character that makes you laugh and whose voice you can mimic.

3. Using the character's voice, repeat over and over the exact words that person in the picture used to say. So if it's a picture of your mom, who said, "Nice girls are polite to everyone," say this over and over in your cartoon character's voice.

4. Repeat the line in the character's voice for sixty seconds.

5. When you're done with that picture, move on to the next one.

6. Keep repeating the assertiveness-related phrases until you've gone through all five pictures.

Hopefully these two defusion activities will help you begin to look at these stressful thoughts, personal scripts, scary pictures, and painful emotions as old, outdated versions of yourself that can be relegated to some trunk in your attic or sack in the corner of your closet. Being more assertive requires practice. You can learn to behave more assertively and update the outdated stressful thoughts, personal scripts, scary pictures, and painful emotions from your past. They don't have to hold you back any longer; you can say no to things that you don't want to do and say yes to the life you want to lead.

THE BLAME GAME

As we've discussed several times in this book, a key aspect of ACT is acceptance. Nowhere is this more important than in accepting and taking responsibility for your feelings. You've probably heard people blame others for their feelings. Perhaps you engage in this blame game yourself by saying things like "She made me feel terrible," "He made me feel guilty," "She made me feel like a jerk," or "He made me feel uncomfortable when he asked me to do that."

Assigning your feelings to others rather than owning up to them is a classic sign of nonassertiveness. Your feelings are your own. No one makes you feel anything. Let me repeat that: no one makes you feel anything. Your feelings are tied to your conceptualized self in a thousand different ways and are tied to the stressful thoughts, personal scripts, scary pictures, and painful emotions that constantly run in the background of that computer-like mind of yours. Perhaps something that someone says or does connects to this material and that triggers an emotional response in your mind, but it's still your mind and your emotional response. You felt the way you did because of your mind, not because of the other person's language or behavior. Blaming others for your negative thoughts and painful emotions is like blaming the weatherman for reporting bad weather.

In order to move forward and ACT to manage your stress, stop blaming others for what you feel and take responsibility for it. From an ACT perspective, it's not helpful to blame others for what you're thinking or feeling. It doesn't help you move forward—and it alienates them.

One way to stop blaming others is to defuse from the blame game whenever you catch yourself playing it. The following simple activity, The Blame Game, can help you defuse from unhelpful, nonassertive, blaming behavior.

DEFUSION ACTIVITY: The Blame Game

Whenever you catch yourself blaming others for your feelings, stop and say to yourself: *My mind is playing the old blame game again. This isn't helping me be assertive.*

Turn your blaming language into song lyrics for the famous Aretha Franklin hit *You Make Me Feel Like a Natural Woman*. (If you aren't familiar with the song, you can look it up on any popular Internet song search engine.) Instead of finishing the song with "feel like a natural woman," insert whatever you're blaming the other person for feeling. For example, if you're blaming someone else for feeling angry, end the song with "you make me feel so angry." Really camp it up. Use something as a microphone prop and really belt it out at the top of your lungs. Elongate the "feeeelllll" and repeat your lyric over and over for a couple of minutes.

For extra effect, play the original song in the background and sing along, inserting your blaming feelings. For a little comic relief, sing the song in the voice of your favorite cartoon character while using the same intensity. The campier you get, the more ridiculous it should seem to you that blaming someone else for what you're feeling will help you in your efforts to be more assertive.

USE "I" LANGUAGE TO TAKE RESPONSIBILITY

If you're feeling stressed by what you consider to be someone's aggressive verbal or physical behavior, it's your responsibility to bring it to their attention. You're the one with the problem. It's bothering you, not them. You can't assume that they have any idea how their comments or behavior are affecting you. The other person may or may not be aware of the effects their behavior or comments have on you. Even if the other person is aware of the effects and is intentionally trying to take advantage of you, it's still *your* responsibility to let that person know what you're thinking and feeling.

The best way to show the other person you're taking responsibility to clear up the problem is by using *I-language*. When you use I-language, you take responsibility for your feelings and do not blame the other person for making you feel that way.

For example, imagine that your friend is explaining to you how to use a few key features of a new cell phone you just bought. Halfway through her explanation, your eyes glaze over and your mind goes totally blank. When she's finished, you still don't understand how to use the features. Besides being confused about how to use your new phone, you're really annoyed at your friend for making things more confusing for you and wasting your precious time with her long-winded explanation about how to use the phone. You say to her, "You really make me mad when you don't explain things clearly." Of course this puts her on the defensive and she replies, "Well, if you weren't such a technological Neanderthal, you'd have understood and not gotten so upset with me." You go back and forth a couple more rounds, and both of you are now angry and blaming the other for it.

Rather than blame your friend for feeling annoyed, you could say, "I am so annoyed by not being able to understand my new phone. These things get more confusing every year." By stating things this way, you own up to your feelings and state them in I-language form. It's important to describe both the situation and your feelings about what happened in clear, simple terms.

LIVING THE LIFE YOU VALUE BY BEING ASSERTIVE

Throughout this book, you've spent a lot of time thinking about your values and the goals you've set for yourself. You've seen how your mind constantly churns out stressful thoughts, personal scripts, scary pictures, and painful emotions that can act as barriers to keep you from achieving your goals and staying true to your values. You've also seen how ACT revolves around helping you break down these barriers and keep moving forward in your attempts to reach your goals.

In the last chapter, we talked about how demands and stimulation relate to your goals. Assertiveness can be a tremendous asset in helping you rid yourself of unwanted demands so you can take on all of the challenging things you need to accomplish in order to meet your goals.

Being assertive means being true to your values. Remember, assertive people know who they are and what they need and want in order to be happy and live life to the fullest. When you behave assertively, you're simply translating your values into action. The more you do this, the easier it gets. The more you stay true to your values through assertive behavior, the less stressed you will be, because there will be no discrepancy between what you value and how you live your life.

CHAPTER 11

ACTing to Manage Your Stress

Now that we've come to the final chapter of this book, I hope, among other things, that you've learned how important your values are. Living out your values is the key not only to managing your stress but also to being the person you most deeply want to be. As you've seen, ACT can be a valuable tool in this process because it reminds you that you are more than the content of your life. Your stressful thoughts, personal scripts, scary pictures, and painful emotions are like pages in the scrapbook of your life. You're the scrapbook—always evolving and adding new chapters. Now you're embarking on a new chapter in your life, one that is purposeful and guided by what you value and is truly important to you.

From today on, you'll start to view your stressful thoughts, personal scripts, scary pictures, and painful emotions as pages in your scrapbook from an earlier time in your life—and you'll recognize that these "pages" don't work for you anymore. They're still in your book but are beginning to fade and turn yellow. Rather than try to remove or change them, you're going to keep them. But even as you keep those old pages, you'll begin to add new pages with more helpful thoughts, valid personal scripts, helpful and inspiring mental images, and acceptance of the full range of emotions that make you human.

In the remainder of this chapter, I'd like to revisit some of the key concepts and strategies that you've learned in this book. This will reinforce how you can use this information and these skills to manage your stress for the rest of your life.

ACCEPTING STRESS

You're a different person today than you were when you first picked up this book. As a result of reading it, you've realized that up until this point in your life, you've probably focused most of your attention on trying to eliminate stress. This is probably why most of what you've tried hasn't worked. Now you can see that focusing most of your attention and energy on trying to eliminate stress actually makes stressful thoughts and emotions worse.

Accepting stress doesn't mean giving up on your efforts to manage your stressors. It doesn't mean wanting to feel tense, anxious, or anything else that the stress response triggers in your body. Accepting stress means that you realize that it's a normal part of your life and that the goal of your stress management activities from this day forward is not to eliminate stress but to learn how to live with it. This means acknowledging and accepting the stressors that are part of your life. It means understanding which of these stressors are based on stressful thoughts, outdated personal scripts, scary pictures, or painful emotions that no longer work for you and then taking steps to work on this. And finally, accepting stress means moving forward in your life while coexisting with the remaining stressors that come along on the journey that is your life.

CLARIFYING YOUR VALUES

ACTing to manage your stress begins with clarifying what you value in life. This is the hard, introspective work that most people avoid. Yet this exciting work couldn't be more relevant and personal. It's your chance to really look within and find your passion. Living a life that springs from the fires inside is what you deserve and can achieve. You've already done this through the values clarification activities earlier in this book. You're so far ahead of the average person in understanding your stress because you've already done the hard work of finding your passion—the passion that your values reveal.

ACTing to manage your stress from this point on involves staying true to the values you've uncovered as you worked your way through this book. It involves setting concrete goals and objectives that reflect your values and periodically assessing your progress. It means being mindful of people, situations, and commitments that can sidetrack you from staying true to your values, interfere with meeting your goals, and create stress. It also involves using your newfound assertiveness skills to say no to the people and situations that will sidetrack you.

ACTing to manage your stress involves resisting the urge to move in directions that take you away from your values and doing what you need to do in order to meet your goals. On your journey, you'll constantly be bombarded by people and situations that conflict with your values and interfere with meeting your goals. This is where you need to take an ACT view and always come back to the key question: Does this help or hinder me in meeting my goals? Asking yourself this question will always center you and put you back in touch with what you value and what you need to do. It will trigger that new personal script that is now operating in the background of your mind, the one that you just created by reading this book. The new script is the one that features you, armed with your new stress-management skills, moving forward in your life while coexisting with your troubles.

CHARTING YOUR COURSE

Clarifying your values leads directly to setting goals and objectives for your life. I like to think of this as charting the course of your life. As an academic, my work life is comprised of semesters—discrete little chunks of time. For each semester, I have goals and objectives, things I want to accomplish in the classroom. I've found that carrying this over to my personal life has been very rewarding and has helped keep me on course to meet my goals. I use five-year chunks of time (versus semesters) to structure my goals and objectives for my personal life.

While I admit that this is tedious work, I urge you to not overlook putting your goals and objectives down on paper according to whatever time frame works for you. Most people don't do this. If they set goals at all, they keep them in their heads and don't put them on paper. I've found that this leads to ambiguity, which is a great source of stress for most of my students and clients. Writing things down, and paying attention to the details, can help you clear up ambiguous goals.

As you've seen throughout this book, putting your thoughts on paper also allows you to step away from them. I'm convinced that this simple act helps you defuse from them and allows you to see them for what they are: your thoughts. Take the time to write your goals and objectives down. It's time well spent and will allow you to look at them more objectively.

BEING WILLING TO MOVE FORWARD WHILE COEXISTING WITH YOUR STRESS

Once you've charted your course, you've got to start moving forward. Most people spin their wheels a lot but never move forward. They're too afraid. They get so stuck in trying to control all of the variables that could possibly affect their course of action that they fail to do the most important thing— act. You know these people. They're your father, mother, brother, cousin, the guy next door, the woman behind the counter at the diner, the person sitting next to you on the bus. They're the people who start sentences by saying things like "If only I had…," "I could have…," "I should have…," "I wish I had…, "When I was your age…," or "If I only had…."

I call this "coulda, woulda, shoulda" language. It's kind of sad to hear these laments. Many of these people got stuck trying to control everything rather than just moving forward. Acting to manage your stress involves moving forward once you've charted your course. You know that you'll encounter stressors along the way. You know that you'll be carrying some baggage from your past. You've learned some defusion techniques for helping you drop some of the baggage and coexist with the rest.

Moving forward while coexisting with your stressful thoughts, personal scripts, scary pictures, and painful emotions is hard to do. It's much easier to just avoid it or take some drug to deaden the pain, so I'm not going to delude you into thinking this journey will be easy. I know from personal experience, however, that the pain is worth it. I also know that it gets easier to coexist with your stress and pain over time. It took me a year to wean myself completely off of Xanax for my anxiety after reading the ACT book *The Worry Trap*, by Chad LeJeune (2007). I had to learn how to coexist with the pain and suffering of anxiety and worry without relying on medication. It took a while. It wasn't easy, but if I can do it, so can you.

MANAGING CONTROL ISSUES

Giving up control is scary. It involves having faith that your stress will get better if you accept your stressors and stop trying to control them. I'm sure the first time you read this earlier in the book you were skeptical, to say the least. By now, you realize that most of your stress is caused by things that you can't control. You understand that your mind has the ability to crank out those pesky internal potential stressors (stressful thoughts, personal scripts, scary pictures, and painful emotions) at the most inopportune times. You also realize that trying to control them is futile and can actually make them worse.

You've learned that it's much more productive to shift your attention to things that you can control, such as your behavior and your environment. While you can't control a stressful thought or painful emotion once it's triggered, you can engage in behaviors that will trigger positive thoughts and uplifting emotions. For example, if you know that going for a run usually makes you feel great and triggers a surge of optimism, you can go for a run when you're stressed out. Rather than focusing on the negative aspects of the stress, you can start running and be more mindful of the experience of running. When you're fully into your run, you experience each breath, each contraction of your leg muscles, each stride anew and revel in the exhilaration of this experience.

You've also learned that your microenvironment, that immediate context in which you spend most of your time, can add to your stress or help control it. As you saw earlier, something as common as your commute to work can greatly impact your stress. The time you spend on your commute and the specific nature of how you get there are things you can control. When you begin to ACT to manage your stress, you're mindful of the effects of environmental conditions like this on your life and your stress. You don't merely accept what others have to say about the experience. You pay attention to the effects of the commute on your life and take steps to modify it if it becomes a source of stress.

There are also little things you can do to make your environment (your car, your home, your office, or whatever) a source of comfort rather than stress. Simple things like adding beauty or creature comforts can make your microenvironment a refuge from the crazy, stressful world. Putting flowers on your table, playing relaxing music in the background, and adding sensual aromas by burning candles and incense are simple examples of little things you can do to enhance your environment. Adding small things like this to your environment can bring a sense of peace, beauty, and calm into your inner sanctum.

STOPPING TO SMELL THE ROSES: BEING MORE MINDFUL

Mindfulness is a thread that runs through this book and is a key aspect of ACTing to manage your stress. As you've seen, paying more attention, on purpose, to what is going on inside of you and in your immediate environment is a skill that you can learn. Informal and formal mindfulness practice will help you become more aware of your potential stressors and your ability to manage them.

You can't accept your stressful thoughts, personal scripts, scary pictures, and painful emotions unless you're aware of them. The more you can focus your full attention on these things, the easier it is to accept them and move forward. The same is true for the bodily sensations associated with the stress response. Being more mindful of the stress signals your body sends (muscle tension, feeling jumpy or edgy, and so on) can help you intervene more rapidly and effectively. I'm sure you know someone who ignores such warning signs and walks around with chronic tension, muscle pain, or other physical symptoms and isn't even aware these may represent chronic stress.

Mindfulness also is a key ingredient of coping. It is central to all ACT techniques. Defusion techniques revolve around defusing from stressful thoughts, outdated personal scripts, scary pictures, and painful emotions. In order to defuse from these things, you first have to be aware of their presence and be able to identify them. Being more mindful is a key component of meditation and all of the relaxation strategies you've learned in this book.

ACTing to manage your stress requires that you continue to not only practice informal and formal mindfulness but also that you incorporate these into your daily lifestyle. In this sense, you don't look at mindfulness as a skill but rather a way of being. When this happens, you simply become a more mindful person, not someone who practices mindfulness.

DEFUSING WHEN YOU GET STUCK

Perhaps nothing characterizes ACTing to manage your stress more fully than the notion of getting unstuck. I hope you love this about ACT as much as I do—the notion that you (and I) are not crazy, just stuck. This makes ACT so forgiving and kind as a form of therapy. I hope you find this liberating and that you can now stop calling yourself whatever diagnosis (neurotic, clinically depressed, or whatever) someone slapped on you in order to bill your health insurance carrier. You are not the problem: you are just a person who is stuck and who needs to develop more psychological flexibility.

Practicing the defusion techniques I've offered in this book on a regular basis is an excellent way to ACT on managing your stress. They are unique and offer you a simple way to defuse from and coexist with all the wild and crazy things your mind has conjured up that cause you stress. Being able to separate the things that go on in your mind to create stress from you, the person, is a key facet of ACTing to manage your stress—as is understanding that distinction. You're a wonderful collection of flesh and blood, experience, accomplishment, relationships, dreams, and a thousand other things. From this point on in your life, I want you to start acknowledging this "you" and start giving yourself more credit for being the terrific person that you are.

STAYING TRUE TO YOUR OPTIMAL LEVEL OF STIMULATION AND DEMAND

Only you know how much and what kind of stimulation and demand you need in order to enjoy your life and perform at peak efficiency. Just as there are no universal stressors that fit everyone under all circumstances, there is no universal level of stimulation and demand that applies for all people. A key component of ACTing to manage your stress is finding this out for yourself. As you've learned, the only way to find out what is optimal is to push beyond it and then readjust.

I'm not so concerned with your performing at your absolute peak efficiency as much as I am with your taking on too much and getting stressed. When you take on too many things, these activities become stressors and start to make your life miserable. If you prefer to function at a high level but not strive for peak performance, that's perfectly okay—it's your choice. At this level, the activities you engage in are enjoyable or tolerable and not a source of stress.

When you ACT to manage your stress, you take responsibility for finding your optimal level of stimulation and demand. This involves knowing what kind of stimuli and level of demand you need to live a life in harmony with your values and goals. It also involves backing out of commitments when you've taken on too many things and your performance and your satisfaction with life start to suffer. And finally, it means being asser-tive in sticking to your optimal level when others make excessive demands on you.

DE-STRESSING THROUGH RELAXATION

If you're serious about ACTing to manage your stress, you'll make relax-ation a priority and a regular part of your lifestyle. I always tell my clients and students that I put at least thirty minutes of relaxation a day down as an A-list activity when managing my time. If I can't fit in at least thirty minutes to do something that is both relaxing and fun, then I've got to cut back on other commitments.

I don't need to tell you how important it is to practice the relaxation strategies you've learned in this book on a regular basis. You probably bought this book because you were feeling the effects of stress (muscle tension, nervous energy, and so on) and wanted to learn how to relax more effectively. Now that you know the key elements of true relaxation, practice them until you're comfortable performing them. Build them into your life so they're part of your daily routine. Get to the point where you simply won't allow the presence of tension or other stress symptoms to continue once you become aware of them. For example, rather then go to bed feeling tense, take the time to perform one of the relaxation techniques in this book to release the tension. When you're really ACTing to manage your stress, you'll make relaxation a part of all of your daily experiences. Whether you're at work, at home, on vacation, or traveling, you'll build in a way to breathe, meditate, or use visualization to refresh yourself and reduce your stress. You won't feel awkward doing this. You won't feel uncomfortable explaining what you're doing to others. You'll simply view these activities as part of your life and something you value.

BECOMING A LIFELONG LEARNER

ACTing to manage your stress is a lifelong commitment. If you practice the strategies and skills in this book, learning how to manage your stress should get easier over time. Life experience and regular practice are great teachers. You can use the information of your life experience and practice to make better judgments regarding the threat involved in potential stressors and your ability to cope with them. I always tell my clients and students that one advantage of being fifty-eight years old is having all of that life experience to draw on. When I look at potential stressors and my ability to cope with them, I can look back at similar experiences and past successes to help me make better stress appraisals. You can do the same thing if you make the commitment to keep practicing the techniques learned in this book and to keep an open mind. You can constantly reinvent yourself and learn new things if you allow yourself to.

If you take an ACT view on lifelong learning about managing your stress, you realize that your mind will continue to develop new thoughts, personal scripts, mental images, and emotions. Many of these can be positive, empowering tools that will help you expand your ability to accurately judge potential stressors and your ability to cope with them.

That's it—there's nothing more to say. Follow these simple guidelines. Everything you need for each of the steps is contained within this book. All you need to do is practice and keep moving forward. Good luck and enjoy your journey!

References

Anderson Krech, L., and G. Krech. 2003. Exercises and Daily Journal: Residential Certification Program in Japanese Therapies. ToDo Institute: Monkton, VT.

Ardell, D. 1985. *The History and Future of Wellness*. Dubuque, IA: Kendall/ Hunt.

Benson, H. 1975. *The Relaxation Response*. New York: Avon Books.

Blonna, R. 2006. *Seven Weeks to Conquering Your Stress*. Charleston, SC: BookSurge Publishing.

Blonna, R. 2007. *Coping with Stress in a Changing World*. 4th ed. New York: McGraw-Hill.

Delongis, A., J. C. Coyne, G. Dakof, S. Folkman, and R. S. Lazarus. 1982. Relationship of Daily Hassles, Uplifts, and Major Life Events to Health Status. *Health Psychology* 1 (2):119–36.

Dunn, H. 1962. High-Level Wellness in the World of Today. *Journal of the American Osteopathic Association* 61:9.

Elkins, J. 2000. *How to Use Your Eyes*. New York: Routledge.

Frankenhaeuser, M. 1983. The Sympathetic-Adrenal and Pituitary-Adrenal Responses to Challenge: Comparison between the Sexes. In *Biobehavioral Bases of Coronary Heart Disease*, ed. T. M. Dembroski and D. Blumchen. Basel, Switzerland: Karger.

Germer, C. K. 2005. Mindfulness: What Is It? Does It Matter? In *Mindfulness and Psychotherapy*, ed. C. K. Germer, R . Siegel, and P. Fulton. New York: Guilford Press.

Goleman, D. 1997. *Emotional Intelligence*. New York: Bantam Books.

Harris, R. 2007. *The Happiness Trap*. Boston: Trumpeter Books.

Hayes, S. C. 1984. Making Sense of Spirituality. *Behaviorism* 12:99–110.

Hayes, S. C. 1994. Content, Context, and the Types of Psychological Acceptance. In *Acceptance and Change: Content and Context in Psychotherapy*, ed. S. C. Hayes, N. S. Jacobson, V. M. Follette, and M. J. Dougher, 13–32. Reno, NV: Context Press.

Hayes, S. C. 2001. Acceptance, Mindfulness, and Science. *Clinical Psychology: Science and Practice* 9 (1):101–106.

Hayes, S. C. 2004a. Acceptance and Commitment Therapy, Relational Frame Therapy, and the Third Wave of the Behavioral and Cognitive Therapies. *Behavior Therapy* 35 (4):639–65.

Hayes, S. C. 2004b. Interview by New Harbinger Publications. www .newharbinger.com/client/client_pages/monthinterview_HAYES.cfm.

Hayes, S. C. 2005. *Get Out of Your Mind and Into Your Life: The New Acceptance and Commitment Therapy*. Oakland, CA: New Harbinger.

Hayes, S. C. 2007. Interview by David Van Nuys, Ph.D. July 23, 2007. From the podcast series "The Wise Counsel." www.mentalhelp.net/poc /view_doc.php?type=doc&id=13056&cn=91.

Hayes, S. C., D. Barnes-Holmes, and B. Roche. 2001. *Relational Frame Theory: A Post-Skinnerian Account of Human Language and Cognition*. New York: Plenum.

Holmes, T., and Rahe, R. 1967. The Social Readjustment Rating Scale. *Journal of Psychosomatic Research* 11:213–18.

Krech, G. 2005. Resource materials from Working with Your Attention, a distance learning program through ToDo Institute, Monkton, VT.

Lazarus, R. S., and S. Folkman. 1984. *Stress Appraisal and Coping*. New York: Springer.

LeJeune, C. 2007. *The Worry Trap*. Oakland, CA: New Harbinger.

Luoma, J. B., S. C. Hayes, and R. D. Walser. 2007. *Learning ACT: An Acceptance and Commitment Therapy Skills-Training Manual for Therapists*. Oakland, CA: New Harbinger.

Nhat Hanh, Thich. 1991. *Peace Is Every Step: The Path of Mindfulness in Everyday Life*. New York: Bantam Books.

Polk, K. 2008. ACT Gone Wild. Preconference workshop at the ACT IV meeting, Chicago, IL.

Seligman, M. 1990. *Learned Optimism*. New York: Free Press.

Selye, H. 1956. *The Stress of Life*. New York: McGraw-Hill.

Simon, S. B., L. W. Howe, and H. Kirschenbaum. 1995. *Values Clarification: A Practical, Action-Directed Workbook*. New York: Warner Books.

World Health Organization. 1947. Constitution of the World Health Organization. *Chronicles of the World Health Organization* 1:29–43.

Richard Blonna, Ed.D., is university professor at William Paterson University of New Jersey and a nationally certified life coach, counselor, and health education specialist. He has taught and written about stress management for over twenty years, helping thousands of students and clients learn how to manage their stress using his holistic approach. Blonna lives in Hillsborough, NJ. Visit him online at www.healthystressdoctor.com.

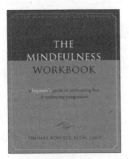
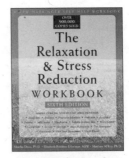